THE ESTABLISHMENT CLAUSE
AND "THE CITY ON A HILL"

THE ESTABLISHMENT CLAUSE AND "THE CITY ON A HILL"

Frank Schneider Jr

To order additional copies of this book, contact:
Xlibris Corporation
1-888-795-4274
www.Xlibris.com
Orders@Xlibris.com
39002

Contents

Foreword

The purpose here is not to recall selected events in our Nation's history; rather, the intent is to add a small voice to refute the powerful secular message increasingly heard throughout our land, and to point to the source or America's greatness that has been shaped by a Higher Power. The events and outcomes herein cited should reinforce an understanding that we today, as did early Christians, saw God at work in the whole culture—not merely written in stone, but in the hearts of men.

Historians agree that the creation of the United States of America should be considered the greatest of all human events, the central development in the history of the world, and the greatest of all human adventures. America was not invented by our Founding Fathers in Philadelphia in 1787, nor did it begin with the first permanent English settlement at Jamestown, VA, in 1607. It began more deeply in the past, beyond our English heritage and European background, the Protestant and Catholic reformations, and all the great civilizations in the history of our world.

It is traditional to refer to America as a Christian nation. At the time of the Revolution religious organizations dominated political developments and served as political parties. The range of Protestant denominations predominated but Catholic churches and Jewish synagogues were well-established. It is recorded that, considering they were in the minority, Jews contributed extensively with financial support and assistance to the cause of the Revolution. They, along with Protestants and Catholics, immigrated to America to escape persecution and seek freedom to worship.

Christians consider the theology set forth in the New Testament as a continuation of that written in the Torah or the Old Testament, to which Christians refer, but both reveal the inspired word of God. From the beginning God has sought to have men learn to know Him and His will for us—namely, as He instructed Abraham, to "Walk before Him". America has opened her arms to all denominations to worship in keeping with their various beliefs, but America is what it is because its roots grew from Judaism and Christianity.

When God created Man, He instilled in him a spirit and soul as two inseparable traits—freedom of choice and need and yearning to worship. Both traits are now validated from DNA and brain-mapping research. This understanding should be seen directly related to the purpose here, along with the evolvement of America as a Judeo-Christian nation, and the peril we face because the *Establishment Clause* to our *Constitution* continues to be rewritten.

Sadly, our Nation today is frequently described as a "Nation Adrift." Nations rise and fall, not from conquers from outside their borders, but from beliefs, practices, and moral decay that evolve over time from within. Our Nation is young and we must appreciate our heritage of religious and political freedom based upon a Biblical understanding of the nature of man and God's blessing in war and peace. As stated elsewhere, our Judeo-Christian faith and morality are under attack by a humanist, secular and atheistic segment of our society that is fervently promoting a "New Morality."

Underscored is the belief that the delinquency of our Nation, lies in great part, at the doors of our judicial system and the quality of state and national judges. The focus of the damage can be traced to the U.S. Supreme Court in 1947 in a series of cases relating to religious practices in public schools—our Nation's Melting Pot," Our primary agency for shaping and nurturing a "City on a Hill."

When our Constitution was ratified our founding fathers did not believe it represented a "perfect union"; rather, because it was created by man, it was only a "more" perfect union. As in maintaining an orrery, (the mechanism that shows the relative position and motion of bodies in the solar system), it would require great discipline and respect for its laws, otherwise it would be wrecked "in short order'.

This book is not intended to be a history, but an historical path is used to show significant mileposts that mark religious influence in shaping a nation that is destined to be, and may yet become, a "City on a Hill."

The story goes, at the time of the Constitutional Convention a lady approached Benjamin Franklin and asked him if the Convention had formed a republic or monarchy". Franklin replied, "Madam, a republic if you can keep it."

Franklin could have replied, but did not of course, "Madam you have a Judeo-Christian nation, if you can keep it."

Chapter 1

A New World is Found

The discovery and exploration of the New World took was beginning as Europe was emerging from the Middle Ages and entering the period we refer to as the Modern Age. This new era was marked by extraordinary changes including growth of commerce and industry, independent nation-states, interest in science, printing, questioning of established authority, and religious unrest.[1]

The evolution of civilization during the classical Period had centered in the Mediterranean Sea and the Near East. The Medieval Period had expanded man's vision to include all of Europe and most of the Old world. The Modern Age, with the advent of printing, expanded man's horizon to cover the whole globe. The feudal system, and the feudal nobility, was on the wane and there was movement to achieve greater cohesion within various national groups. Rulers who favored the new centralization and absolute monarchies came into being that concentrated personal power in their own hands. This "New Monarchy" developed early in Portugal and accounted for her early lead in exploratory voyages to the little known West African Coast where trading posts were established.[2]

Prior to this time Emperor Constantine had placed Christianity on an equal basis with widespread pagan beliefs. This made for a state religion and an ecclesiastical government. Christianity thus spread to east and west Europe and to Rome. It is needful to also note the significance of the emergence of the Islam after 600 A.D. The Prophet Muhammad, an obscure Bedouin herdsman and trader, influenced by Jews and Christians, fathered Islam, which spread rapidly from its birthplace in Mecca to Syria, Persia, Egypt, India and Central Asia.[3]

In 1488, Bartholomew Diaz sailed as far as the southern coast of Africa. Vasco da Gama later rounded the Cape of Good Hope and continued to the eastern coast of Africa into the Indian Ocean and to the Port of Malindi. Extensive trade was carried on between Europe and the East Indies. Products from the East were highly prized in Europe but trade routes by land were costly, expensive and dangerous. With the growing belief that the world was round rather than flat, there was increasing interest in a trade-route by water.[4]

By the middle of the 15th century Spain had pushed the Portuguese from the Canary Islands. As the power of the Portuguese declined, Spain became the mightiest nation in the world and proceeded to build a colonial empire. Spain pioneered transatlantic voyages due too the ambitious, religious and navigational ability of Christopher Columbus. His early experience at sea and his interest in mapmaking, and geography, convinced him that the Indies could be reached by sailing westward. His proposal to attain funds for such a voyage was eventually approved by Spain. His epic five week voyage to the New World with the three ships, Santa Maria, Pint and Nina, became the event that marks the turning point in the history of the world.[5]

Rather than the secular image that he has frequently been portrayed, Columbus was a devout Catholic who drew on the *Bible* for his geographic theories. European Christians felt hemmed in by the wealth and power of Muslims, their expansionist faith, and their control of lucrative trade routes. Columbus was inspired to recruit the "Asians" to Christianity, use them in war against Muslims and reclaim Jerusalem.[6] On the 8th of October, 1492, Columbus recorded a sighting of land birds and stated, "Thanks be to God." Earlier, in an effort to instill "good hopes" in his complaining sailors, he noted that he "had to go to the Indies and would go until he found them "with the help of the Lord."[7]

His moving, prayerful testament, ser in his diary, should convince of Columbus's Christian faith.

> It was the Lord who put into my mind. I could feel His hand upon me to believe that it would be possible that I could sail from here to the Indies. All who heard of my project rejected it and laughed and ridiculed me.
>
> There is no doubt that the inspiration was from the Holy Spirit because He comforted me with rays of marvelous inspiration from Holy scriptures—to a most unworthy sinner.

I have cried out to the Lord for grace and mercy and was covered completely and I have found the sweetest consolation and I have made it my whole purpose to employ His marvelous presence.

It is simply the fulfillment of what I dared prophesy, that He would call and carry me to the far islands that the truth of God's Word might be carried. It is a just and intention for His Holy Providence.[8]

Columbus renamed islands he discovered to honor the Spanish royal family or Christian holy days, and adopted his first name as "Christoferens," (Christ-bearer) as a testament to his sense of divine mission. When Columbus set foot on San Salvador 1492, he and his men fell on their knees and gave thanks to God for their safe voyage and planted a cross firmly in the ground.

Although Columbus did not reach Asia he found a source of riches that enabled Christendom to grow more powerful and wealthy than the Moslem world.[9]

Chapter 2

The New World is Colonized

Spanish Colonies and Provinces

Following Columbus's voyages, Spain took the lead in exploring the New World. Spanish monarchs granted tracts of land to favored subjects as early as 1509, and by 1574 there were 200 Spanish provinces, mainly in the West Indies and South America. Control and supervision of Spanish settlements was strict with bureaucratic control that extended to the farthest outposts. Their introduction of foods and goods unique to America became common in Europe and was a factor that later contributed to trade problems between the colonies and England.[10]

Seventy years after Columbus's historical voyage Spain had no permanent settlement in North America, as they did in the West Indies. Provinces there were governed with an iron hand and the Roman Catholic religion was the only one allowed. Indians and imported Negroes were harshly treated as was seen in the European slave trade. The Spanish crown felt entrusted with a divine mission to convert the Indians to Christianity. Ruthless treatment of the Indians was no guarantee to converting them which brought strong objections by the friars and brought about more peaceful persuasion and compromises in religious customs.[11]

Columbus's first Spanish settlement in 1502 was not successful, but Santo Domingo, settled later did survive. After forts were built the first substantial building was the church. Clerics from the Dominican and Franciscan Orders played a major part in the colonizing process and by1512 the first Bishopric in the New World was founded. In addition to finding an alternate route to the Indies, his objective was to bring Christianity to the "Indians," thought to be under the control of Muslims. Columbus' voyage did not end in Asia, but his voyages enabled Christendom to grow more powerful in Europe to counter expanding Islam. Spain later sent missionaries to convert and pacify the Indians.[12]

It is noted that during this period of colonization that Martin Luther, a devout Catholic priest, nailed his ninety-nine theses on the door of all Saints Church in Wittenberg.

As Spain expanded her control in America she relied on the establishment of missions and sent priests to Christianize the Indians and teach them to be obedient subjects to the Spanish throne. Early missions included a church building and living quarters for priests and Indians. Three Orders of Catholic priests and monks, including Franciscans, Dominicans, and Jesuits, were deeply involved in founding missions and promoting the Catholic faith.

Portuguese Colonization

Portugal was the second major power to enter the race to establish an empire in the New World. Their interest, however, was focused on the eastern part of South America. Spain was not interested in the Eastern part of South America but wanted to limit Portuguese claims. Spanish rulers, in 1493, urged Pope Alexander 1V to establish the Papal Line of Demarcation that circled the globe from north to south that separated Spanish and Portuguese claims that were not already claimed by a Christian king. A year later, Spain and Portugal agreed to adjust the line more to the liking of Portugal that resulted in Portuguese claim to Brazil, one of the largest countries in the world. Portugal followed Spain's lead in establishing missions and missionary priests to the end that Brazil's population today is about ninety percent Catholic.[13]

French Colonization

Early in the 16th century French fishermen from La Rochelle had been working the rich fishing grounds of the Grand Banks off Newfoundland and Labrador. In 15343 Jacques Cartier went up the St Lawrence River and made a second trip in 1541 in search for gold and diamonds. The religious wars in Europe motivated the protestant, French Admiral, Gaspard de Coligny, to mount an expedition to colonize an island at Rio de Janeiro. In 1560 the Portuguese attacked the colony and hanged all the inhabitants. French Huguenot colonies at Fort Carolina in Florida and Charles Fort suffered a similar fate in 1565 by the Spanish who erected their own strongholds at St. Augustine and St Catherine's Island. In 1572, Admiral Coligny was murdered in the Massacre of St Bartholomew that ended the early phase of French colonization.

In 1524, the Italian seaman, Giovanni da Verrazano, an Italian explorer, was hired by King Francis I of France to search for a shorter route to "Asia." He sailed to North Carolina and up the coast to Nova Scotia, found no shorter route, but claimed all the land for France.

Ten years later Jacques Cartier discovered the Gulf of St Lawrence but did not succeed in establishing a lasting colony.

Samuel de Champlain, it is believed, should receive the most credit for the colonization and establishment of Quebec in 1608, the seat of the "New France." He believed that France could hold the Indians' friendship by teaching them the Christian religion. In all settlements churches were built and wherever trappers and traders went missionaries followed, or led the way.

France colonies along the St. Lawrence River, around the Great Lakes, down the Mississippi Valley to New Orleans and up the Ohio River to Fort Duquesne, now Pittsburg. As with the Spanish, French settlements were closely supervised with government restrictions that extended conditions in France. French colonies followed Spain's success in building Franciscan missions in Florida and New Mexico to convert Indians and strengthen the fur trade in New France. The dream of a French empire in the New World, however, was not to be realized due to limited emigrants, a semi-feudal system and lack of individual and religious freedom.[14]

Dutch Colonization

The Dutch also sought to exploit the New World resources and extent the power of their home government. In 1609, Henry Hudson, an English sea Captain, was hired by a group of Dutch merchants to search for a northwest passage to Asia. When Henry Hudson reported the potential of Dutch settlements along the Hudson River, the Dutch West Indies Company was organized and granted rights to start trading colonies between the Delaware and Connecticut Rivers. After 1624, Dutch settlers were located at site of present day Albany and Manhattan. Manhattan became the capital of New Amsterdam

The colony that the Dutch established on the Hudson River is viewed as a minor enterprise during the seventeenth century, as the Netherlands emerged as an economic and military giant. The Dutch nation had the most efficient merchant marine and fishing fleet that dominated Western Europe, the North Seas, fisheries and artic whaling. Amsterdam was the preeminent shipping, banking, insurance, printing and textile manufacturing center in all of Europe. While most Europeans countries persecuted religions dissidents and expelled minorities, the Dutch welcomed outcasts, French Protestants and Iberian and German Jews.

Until around 1650 Spain continued to have the only empire of consequence in the Western Hemisphere. Dutch ventures, as other countries, had to consider the power of Spain in any colonizing effort. The Dutch West Indies Company, reorganized in 1621, was interested in striking out at Spain out of religious and national zeal as much as for economic benefits.

Dutch claims were not extensively settled because the land was controlled by landlords and it was difficult for emigrants to own their land. Near the end of the 1500's, the English had helped the Dutch win independence from Spain. The Dutch, successful traders, were now competing with British merchants for trade and naval power, a development that led to armed conflict. When England and Holland went to war in 1664, England seized New Netherlands territory that is now named New York, New Jersey, Pennsylvania and Delaware, and later settled by Puritans and Quakers.[15]

Chapter 3

England's Colonial Empire

The settlement at Jamestown in 1607 was the first permanent English colony and the event that we mark as the end of the colonial era and the beginning of American history. The Virginia Company had not left out the religious element and asserted that its object was to "preach and baptize into the Christian Religion and by propagation of the Gospel, to recover out of the arms of the "Divell," a number "poure" and miserable souls, "wrapt" up unto death, in almost invincible ignorance."[16]

While Spain heretofore enjoyed wealth, military power and profitable trade, England rapidly gained strength from an expanded navy, increased trade, and a significant victory over the Spanish armada in 1588, England gained control of the seas. The spirit of the renaissance promoted rapid progress from feudalism, expanded industry and made for profound changes in intellectual, political and religious freedom.[17]

The Jamestown settlement had a feeble beginning and was disappointing to the trading company that funded the venture. It was intended to be economically profitable and as previous goals of Spain and France, the intention was to spread the Christian faith among the Indians; but in contrast to Spain and France, the Anglican Church was to be the only form of worship. The early settlement suffered one dreadful setback after another, and by 1609 it was at low ebb. However, in 1610, new settlers and fresh supplies saved the colony from failure and abandonment. Some historians have noted that the earlier failures were fortuitous because if the colony had quickly grown and prospered, it would have been taken over by Spain, who controlled the sea in that area.[18]

King James believed that the colony had been mismanaged and annulled the London Company's Charter. It then became a royal colony with supervision by a governor appointed by the king. This governmental system, by 1750, was the pattern followed in most of the colonies: a council chosen by the governor and an assembly elected by freemen of the colony.

Fortunes of the colonies increased when English "cruel laws" were replaced by "free laws", and thus, seeds of democracy were planted. Colonies flourished under self rule and each colony had its own constitution. Still under English control, however, the colonies maintained fear and dislike of government far removed from them. Their attachment for constitutional government was firmly fixed.

English businessmen prospered and had money organized trade companies, such as the Plymouth, London, and Virginia Companies, and secured a King's Charter to invest in colonies on the continent. It is significant to note that this is in contrast to expeditions by other world powers, whose ventures were by kings, England's were funded by private businessmen. Also significant, settlers from England came to America one way or another for individual and religious freedom and came to stay.

There were continuous English colonial settlements from 1607 to 1783, beyond the time the united colonies declared their independence in 1775. A truism is that freedom is the mainspring of human progress and the colonies prospered as the result of new Company policies. Adult settlers were given a share in the Company and an allotment of land that increased production. A variety of products was produced including tobacco, which gained great appeal to Europeans. In 1619 the Virginia Company authorized an assembly to help write laws for the Company and approved two representatives from each settlement. This act is considered to be the beginning of representative government in America.[19]

The Mercantilism (the Navigation or Trade Acts), introduced by Oliver Cromwell, had long been in practice. It was a belief that the colonies existed for the benefit of the mother country. Colonies would supply England with raw materials for manufacture in England and purchase the manufactured goods only from England. Taxes were collected and shipped only in English ships. The colonies were prospering with extensive trade with Europe, Africa, and the West Indies. Goods were transported in ships constructed manned and owned by colonists. England's was with the French had ended, in debt, young King George III was now in power and he determined to strengthen England's economy with closer supervision of the colonies. He acted early to enforce the Navigation Act, which the colonist resorted to by smuggling their goods. English agents were then appointed by the colonial governor to bring smugglers to trial—with rulings by the judges without juries. Colonists considered this practice a violation of their "Rights as Englishmen."[20]

From 1660 for the next 100 years there had been little supervision of the American colonies. The English colonies grew strong and prosperous but the French were developing an empire inland and to the north. In 1608, Samuel de Champlain organized a settlement at Quebec and maintained good relations with the Algonquin and Huron Indians in the Great Lakes area. The relationship between the French and the Indians made a formidable barrier to English expansion. In 1660, when the French king came to the throne, his country assisted the French allies to make war against the Iroquois who were hostile to the French.[21]

The colonists not only defended their local governments and their trade, they also helped their mother country in defending their borders against the French and the Indians, the greater threat coming from the French. The Seven Years War, (that we in America remember as the French and Indian War) was the final struggle. By 1744, the French were continuing their expansion with raids to control the Ohio Valley. The contest for the Ohio Valley is of special interest as it brought George Washington to the stage of American history, and doubtless to provide him with wisdom and military experience for his role in the American Revolution.[22]

In 1753, the French were building a series of forts to connect Lake Erie and the Ohio River. Washington, now a Major in the Virginia militia, was sent to warn he French commanders the territory belonged to the crown of Great Britain. After narrowly escaping assassination by an unfaithful Indian guide, he returned to Williamsburg to file his report. A year later he was sent again to prevent the French from seizing the "forks of the Ohio" where the Allegheny and Monongahela Rivers merge. His skirmish with French and Indians at Great Meadow is considered as the first shots fired in this war that involved three continents. Benefits of the Seven Years War included the lessening of America's dependence on Great Britain and the end of the French threat to further expansion.[23]

America continued to grow from the thirteen colonies planted by England over the course of one hundred and twenty-five years. Understandably, the colonies carried the stamp of England's tumultuous history during the period of the Renaissance, the age of Discovery and the Protestant Reformation. The ending of the French expansion in the New World had left a vacuum into which he English stepped, the time that we date the ultimate origins of the

American people and traced to the exploration of the Labrador coast in 1498. The United States eventually grew from thirteen colonies planted by England over the course of one hundred and twenty-five years. Understandably, the colonies carried the stamp of England's tumultuous history during the periods of the Renaissance, Age of discovery and the Protestant Reformation.[24]

Francis Jennings underscores the great unifying power of the English language and its literature. There were immigrants who spoke other languages but most came under the influence of the King James *Bible*. Language, law, and religion molded the dominant people as Englishmen—and today, Americans.[25]

Chapter 4

The Mayflower Compact

Thirteen years after the founding of Jamestown in 1620 another group of English colonists came to America. The landing of the Mayflower at New Plymouth, later to become Massachusetts, is recorded as one of the most important formative events in American history, and to ultimately bear on the crisis of the American republic. They were mostly Puritans who grew discontent in the Church of England and worked towards religious, moral and societal reforms. The Mayflower men and women came to America not primarily for gain or even livelihood, though they accepted both from God with gratitude, but to create His kingdom on earth.[26]

The writings of John Calvin, a leader in the Reformation, gave rise to Protestantism and were pivotal to the Christian revolt. So dissatisfied with the Church of England that they migrated to Holland to worship, but their unhappiness with the worldly life-style there caused them to found a colony in Virginia. They returned to England in 1620 where they boarded the vessel, the "Mayflower" the ship that carried them to the New World. Two months, and few days later, the little ship, having been blown off course, dropped anchor off the coast of Cape Cod. The landing of the good ship, Mayflower," is remembered as a milestone in the history of America. As the Jamestown settlement is marked for the establishment of the English tradition and heritage in America, the establishment of the Pilgrims in Massachusetts served to shape America as a religious nation.[27]

The significance of the voyage is summarized in the Mayflower Compact. On leaving England the Pilgrims held a contract from the Virginia Company giving rights of self-government, but the document had no standing in Cape

Cod, where they landed. Fortune hunters, (strangers), who also traveled with them threatened to go their own way as soon s the colony was established. The Pilgrims, according to William Bradford, handled the crisis by forming the Mayflower Compact. The ship moved out into deeper water again where the Compact was drawn up to secure unity and provide for a future government. It was signed by forty-one men on November 11, 1620. It included a civic body to provide just and equal laws founded on church teaching with religion and government to be indistinguishable. The Puritans, holding Calvinist beliefs, based the contract upon the original Biblical covenant between God and the Israelites. It later received expressions in John Locke's *Treatise of Civil Government* in 1690, which was so familiar to the men who formulated our *Declaration of Independence* and *Constitution*. It remained in force until their colony was absorbed in 1691 by the Massachusetts Bay Colony.

As noted, in contrast to earlier settlers who immigrated to America for gain and livelihood, the Pilgrims came to pursue religious freedom and to escape the rigid governance of the established Church of England. During the Middle Ages people of all western Europe were members of the Catholic church. Early in the 16th century, the Protestant Reformation began against the Pope and the Roman Catholic Church. Martin Luther, who led the Reformation, denied the supremacy of the Pope, disagreed with Church doctrine and certain practices, along with his insight regarding "justification by faith". His influence is noted in widespread revolts to gain religions freedom as well as political and economic equality.[28]

The Reformation spread to England with religious beliefs and practices advocated by John Calvin and Martin Luther. During the 1530's King Henry VIII, the most notorious king in English history, rejected the Catholic Pope and became head of an independent and official Church of England. As monarch, he commanded a hierarchy of church officials in England and Wales. Religious descent then was considered treason or heresy. Puritans who wanted to reform the church became separatists and organized independent congregations to practice the pure and simple church of Jesus Christ and his apostles without formalism, ceremonies, and dogmas not set forth in the *Bible*.[29]

John Winthrop, noted Pilgrim leader, later wrote of their attempt to build "a city on a hill" never doubted that the colony's affairs were guided by the hand of God. The Mayflower Compact is remarkable in that it is not a document between a people and a king but between like-minded individuals and each other, with God as a witness and symbolic co-signatory. William Bradford, another leader of the group later added that they were not ordinary Pilgrims who would return home, but they sought to set up a new, sanctified country to be a permanent pilgrimage, traveling continually toward a millenarian goal, "a city on a hill". At the heart of the Compact was the undisputed conviction that God must be at the center of all law and order and that law without a mortal base is really no law at all.[30]

Sellers and May point to the story of religion before the Great Awakening as gradually eroding from the originally dominant Puritan-Calvinist strain of Protestant Christianity. In an increasingly self-reliant, optimistic society, it became more difficult to sustain the awful sovereignty of God in favor of a more Deist kindly god. The more sophisticated classes abandoned God but retained outward forms and language of Christianity.[31]

Clarence L. Ver Steeg clarifies developments that diminished the influence of Puritanism and recorded as the period of "Declension" the falling away from the Puritan Commonwealth. He points to New World conditions that consistently modified intellectual expression and adjustment to the New World, and with the collapse of the Puritan Commonwealth in England, it lost its cosmic significance. Despite some latter-day historians who cast a shadow on the overall character of Puritanism, we still visualize their true nature, handed down from early historians. They saw New England as the wellspring of American life—as virtuous, hard-working, of good judgment, upright, unimpeachable motives and the seat of representative government.[32]

Alan Taylor also disagrees with the myth of Declension as it obscures the prodigious and enduring legacy that evolved that showed America as a moral, educated commercial and homogenous people. The *Bible* Commonwealth never collapsed, its leadership never fell; rather, the Commonwealth responded to new values and purposes as conditions changed. Their imprint was left on the English colonies. Their livelihood, their land, labor, trade, their intellectual life, and their emphasis on family values—all directly influenced by the New World environment.[33]

What the Puritans developed in America was a practical common-law orthodoxy. Their heavy reliance on the *Bible* and their preoccupation with platforms, programs of action and schemes of confederation—rather than religious dogmas—fixed the temper of their society, and foreshadowed American political life for centuries to come.[34]

Chapter 5

The Great Awakening

"America was born in a revival of religion," said President Calvin Coolidge. This series of three intense revivals that began around 1730 swept through the American colonies, served as a catalyst that set in motion forces that eventually brought political freedom, and shaped America into the religious nation it was destined to become. The Puritans who settled in New England in 1620 had the goal of establishing a "city on a hill" with the eyes of the people upon them. The Mayflower Compact, named for ship that brought the Puritan emigrants to Provincetown Harbor, became famous as the first plan for self-government written in America, and included obeisance to just and equal laws that were believed to be for the general good of the colony. They influence was great in New England but they eventually broke away from the Church of England due to their belief that worship should be simple and democratic and the *Bible* should be their law.[35]

By 1750, however, Puritans no longer controlled the thinking in New England There were Congregational churches in most towns in Massachusetts, but Baptists, Quakers and some Anglican church members became unhappy in supporting the Puritan church. Ironically, it was an initiative by the Church of England that contributed to the early phase of religious resurgence in the colonies. In 1680, over 600 Anglican churchmen were sent to the colonies who eventually planted more than three hundred Anglican parishes in the Middle colonies and in New England. This Anglican initiative provoked a vigorous response from the colonists who had fled from the formalism and theology of the Anglican Church and feared that it would become the state church in the colonies.[36]

An additional factor that later contributed to the great revival movement was the growing affluence and spirit of independence. England had allowed the colonies to govern themselves, as noted before, and they became rich and materialistic. It would seem that the Puritan dream of a city on a hill would not come to fruition. Although people were not unchurched, their success tended to foster outward holiness but inwardly, falling away from faith and piety. In a letter to the Reverend Thomas Prince, Jonathan Edwards bemoans his concern for the "abatement of liveliness of people's affections in religion." He lauds the spirit of earlier revivals but, "the work seemed to be much more pure, having less of a corrupt mixture."

By mid-18th century, America had experienced rapid growth, increasingly self-governing, and growing richer. The drift toward modernity had steadily eroded the seventeenth-century piety that the settlers had brought to all the early colonies and of which Puritanism was merely the most intense form. Conspicuous forces that influenced the erosion are seen in the new prosperity, less dependence on God, and a growing belief that "right living is OK."[37]

Although the spirit of Puritanism was declining America's religious characteristics were just beginning to mature and define themselves. The "easy" life was reversed by the Great awakening. It failed to revive old fashioned Calvinist doctrines but served to spread other religious doctrines and create a tolerant attitude toward religious differences. As Paul Johnson relates, the specific form of American Christianity, "undogmatic, moralistic rather than credal, tolerant but strong, and all-pervasive of society, was born, and that the Great Awakening was its midwife." It proved to be of vast significance in religion and politics and one of the key events in American history. The series of three Great Awakenings are seen to be the proto-revolution event, the formative moment in American History and making the political drive for independence possible. As John Adams put it: "The Revolution was effected before the war began. It could not have taken place without the religious background."[38]

The religious revivals that followed crossed all religious and sectarian boundaries and transformed the existing European-style churches into American ones and gave a unique flavor to a range of denominations. This formative period preceded the drive for independence and the revolution could not have taken place without it. The birth-spark of the spiritual movement in all areas of the colonies was lit and nourished by fiery, emotional sermons by such men as Theodore Fredinghuysen, pastor of the Dutch reformed church in the Raritan Valley, William Tennent, the Scotch-Irish Presbyterian, who settled at Beshaming, PA, around 1720, Jonathan Edwards, a minister at the Congregational church in Northampton, MA, John Wesley, Methodist minister in Georgia, George Whitefield, who ignited "violent sheets of religious sheets of religious flames from Savannah to Boston," and John Davenport, who became famous for his outdoor camp meetings.[39]

Knowledge of American history should help us to agree with George Washington, Benjamin Franklin, and Abraham Lincoln, to increasingly see the providence of God behind the events of their days. The nation did not unfold by accident or happenstance, but by divine design.[40]

Chapter 6

America Becomes a Nation

At the end of the French and Indian war, set forth in European history as the seven Years war, the inhabitants of British North America considered themselves loyal and patriotic British subjects. The British Navigation laws had fostered their prosperity; they enjoyed British protection, and came to believe that their political rights and liberties were the same as British rights and liberties. There was no threat now to the freedom of religion they cam to America to enjoy.

When England became aware of competition from the colonies she began tighten her imperial control of the colonies. England needed money to pay war debts and funds to pay the costs of an expanding empire. It seemed fair that the colonies, virtually untaxed, should share England's burden.

The British Parliament Navigation Act had been in effect to restrict and collect customs, but in 1764, under King George III, there was insistence that they be strictly enforced. The intent was to ensure that the colonies traded only with England. George Greenville, British prime minister from 1763 to 1765, inaugurated the first of a series or onerous taxes and regulations that fostered rebellion and the eventual revolution.[41]

The Currency Act of 1764

Included in the several measures was the *Proclamation of 1763* to close frontier lands west of the Appalachians; followed by the *Currency Act of 1764* that forbade the colonies from issuing paper money; The *Revenue Act of 1764*, which included the *Molasses Act of 1733*, but had not been strictly enforced, and levied import duties for revenue rather than for overall trade.

The new rigorous enforcement of the *Molasses Act* had a crippling effect on New England's commerce.

The Stamp Act of 1765

English pressure on the colonists increased when, in 1765, the English Parliament passed Greenville's *Stamp Act* that required colonists to affix stamps to a range of legal and commercial documents. Colonists considered this more "taxation without representation." Their response was violent and resulted in mobs destroying stamps, and expelling tax collectors.[42]

In 1765, John Adams recorded in his diary the growing mood and spirit of he colonists regarding their liberty, and specifically, the *Stamp Act*.

> The *Stamp Act* has raised and spread through the whole continent a spirit that will be recorded to our honor with future generations. The people, even to the lowest ranks, have become more attentive to their liberties, more inquisitive about them, and more determined to defend them. So triumphant is the Spirit of Liberty everywhere. Such a union was never before known in America.[43]

After colonial merchants began to boycott English goods the *Stamp Act* was repealed a year later, but not before the emergence of secret societies called "Sons of Liberty" in every colony.

The Townshend Acts of 1767

The colonists had increasingly learned to rule themselves and rejected all kinds of English taxes. The English Parliament, however, was not willing to surrender its right to legislate for the colonies in all ways. On July 2, 1767, Parliament approved the *Townshend Acts*, named for the Chancellor of the Exchequer, that placed taxes on items that had not been previously taxed before, such as glass tea, paper and printers ink. The colonists, now becoming more American, resorted to mob action, and boycott of all English goods. After customs officers were attacked by mobs in Boston additional troops were sent to subdue the protesting crowd and were fired upon by General Gage's soldiers, the incident that took place in March 1770, is now remembered as the "Boston Massacre" and moved Parliament to repeal all *Townshend Acts* except the tax on tea. Over the next few years there were other acts of violence that caused Lord North to repeal them, with the exception of the tax on tea.[44]

The relative period of peace that followed is thought to have deceived the British ministers, because the colonists were becoming more committed to local government and no "taxes without representation." The Townshend "controversy" was settled, but such "radicals" as Patrick Henry, John Hancock, Samuel Adams and Christopher Gadsden continued to agitate against the duty on tea. Their group had created an organization termed "Committees of Correspondence" with chapters in every colony with the objective of alerting the several colonies of their loss of rights to Britain.

Boston Tea Party

The consumption of tea in the colonies left the British East India Company with a surplus of tea and Lord North, then Tory prime minister, thought that tea could be sold at a cheaper price in the colonies, so, Parliament excused the East India Company from paying the usual export duty. The British Parliament considered the tea tax to be a token one, but to the colonists it was a matter of principle. Tea that was subsequently shipped to Charleston, New York and Philadelphia were either rejected or confiscated. Meetings in Boston also determined that the tea should be shipped back but the colonial governor there refused to allow it. This may account for the action of the "Sons of Liberty, to disguise themselves as Indians and dump tea into the Boston harbor valued at eighteen thousand English pounds."

The Intolerable Acts

In response to the Boston Tea Party, Parliament passed, in 1774, what our history has labeled the *Intolerable Acts*. All of the colonies were affected but Massachusetts was targeted for special punishment. One provision allowed officers representing the British government, accused of serious offences, could be tried in England rather than in the colonies. Another gave the colonial governor power to force citizens to quarter soldiers in their homes. A third act disallowed town meetings. Included in the Act was the requirement that the port of Boston would be closed until the lost tea was paid for. Added in the *Intolerable Acts* was the *Quebec Act* that widened the boundaries of French Quebec to the Ohio River. The colonists objected to the French language and its autocratic form of government. This was another Act of the British Parliament that angered the colonists. It was not to punish the colonists but to update the *Proclamation of 1763* that placed the country north of the Ohio River under the province of Quebec. It assured religious freedom to

Catholics but governed by an appointed council. It was all the more reason for the growing resistance to England and prompted the forming of the First Continental Congress.

First Continental Congress

Britain's retaliatory measures angered not only the Massachusetts colony but all the colonies, as well, and in Spring 1774, the colonies were united in their demand for a general congress. In defiance of Gov. John Murray, Fourth Earl of Dunmore's orders, the Burgesses of Virginia met and proclaimed day of fasting, humiliation and prayer on the day the Boston Harbor would be closed. They favored combined efforts to resist British policies and actions. Encouraged by such sympathy the Massachusetts legislature resolved that a continental congress was highly expedient, invited delegates from all the colonies to meet in Philadelphia on September 5, 1774. Except for Georgia, all the colonies were represented. Opinions of the delegates varied widely, but a compromise was struck. Expressions of loyalty were formulated and sent to the King with a resolution that declared the *Intolerable Acts* were "null and void." Included in the actions of the Congress was the organization of an Association, made up of all the colonies that forbade trade with Britain, with representatives in each colony to see that the boycott orders were enforced. What the First Continental Congress accomplished was important, but the creation of the Association is believed to be the most significant. It became the touchstone by which loyalty to the King or to the colonies was determined.[45]

The *Intolerable Acts* welded the colonies more firmly together and motivated them to assist Boston and resume the ban on importation of English goods. The Congress had agreed to meet again in a year if Britain did not heed their petitions and protests. The British government responded to the demands of the Congress stating willingness to relieve them of any taxation if they would share Britain's defense expenses, provide money to support British officers in the colonies as well as other acts that would cripple colonial commerce. Britain's response also included measures to tighten up efforts to compel obedience to Britain's authority.

When the Congress adjourned there was a belief, particularly in Massachusetts, that war was eminent. A provincial government in Massachusetts assumed the reins of government, began preparing for defense and companies were started to raise volunteers for their militia. Sir Thomas Gage, then Governor of Massachusetts, proceeded to fortify Boston and made plans to confiscate military stores that colonists were collecting.[46]

Second Continental Congress

There was no doubt now that a second conference was needed and one was convened in Independence Hall on May 10, 1775, three weeks after the clashes at Lexington and Concord, where plans were made for possible war. A respectful petition was formulated and sent to King George III which he refused to receive. He responded to the actions of the Second Continental Congress by branding its leaders as rebels and traitors and ordered the "insurrection" to be suppressed.

The Congress further resolved to raise money for war materials, open diplomatic relations with European countries and pledged to persevere until American demands were met or to win independence. Militiamen who were already available were organized into a regular army and George Washington was appointed Commander of the American forces in Massachusetts.[47]

John Adams' autobiography describes the setting when the Congress approved Washington as Commander of what then became the Continental Army. He regarded the 43-year-old Virginia planter as modest, virtuous, amiable, generous and brave. He was chosen in the face of considerable opposition, only because most of the army was at that time from New England. Washington was sitting near the door when he heard Adams allude to him in his presentation and, from his usual modesty, darted into the library room. Opposition to Washington's selection was discussed and later withdrawn as voices were generally so clearly in high favor of him. He was nominated by Thomas Johnson of Maryland and unanimously elected and the Army adopted.[48]

Although only a minority of Americans supported the aggressive tactics of the Continental Association, its radical element held sway in the face of the British plan to eliminate insubordination in Massachusetts. It would seem that the colonists had to continue to resist or submit to the increasing British threat to their independence. Additional troops were sent to Boston under the command of Gen. Thomas Gage who would serve as military governor. The Continental Congress then approved the establishment of a provincial government and began to train troops and collect military supplies.[49]

On the day the Second Continental Congress met, Ethan Allan and a group of men from Vermont, the "Green Mountain Boys" as they called themselves, attacked and captured Forts Ticonderoga and Crown Point on Lake Champlain. They seized artillery and supplies that were later used in the siege on Boston. It is noted that when Allan demanded that the surprised British commander surrender, Allan thundered, "In the name of the Great Jehovah and the Continental Army."[50]

When General Gage became aware that minutemen were being trained and arms and powder had been stored, he sent British soldiers from Boston to Concord to commandeer the stores, and arrest Samuel Adams and John Hancock. Warned by Paul Revere and William Dawes, Jr., "minutemen" assembled at Lexington "on the green." When British forces arrived, Major John Pitcairn, who was in charge of the American force, saw that armed resistance was futile, he ordered his men to disperse. However, as they were breaking ranks, a shot was fired, followed by a skirmish in which the first blood was shed. Who actually fired the shot has been long debated, but that that first shot, fired in April 1775, is regarded as the "shot heard around the world."

The British troops were successful in destroying the stores at Concord but on the return march to Boston they were followed with intense fire from behind buildings and fences by minutemen who were waiting. British troops were rescued by a relieving force but were sent them back to Boston with losses as 273 dead, wounded and missing. Accounts of this event caused a burst of patriotic indignation that, a month later, a Second Continental Congress was assembled in Philadelphia.[51]

Ralph Waldo Emerson has memorialized this event with his *Concord Hymn*, sung at the completion of the Battle Monument on July 4, 1837:

> *By the rude bridge that arched the flood*
> *Their flag to April's breeze unfurled,*
> *Here once the embattled farmers stood*
> *And fired the shot heard round the world.*
> *The foe long since in silence slept;*
> *Alike the conqueror silent sleeps;*
> *And Time the ruined bridge has swept*
> *Down the dark stream which seaward creeps,*
> *On this green bank, by this soft stream,*
> *We set today a votive stone;*
> *The memory may their deed redeem,*
> *When, like our sires, our sons are gone.*
> *Spirit, that made those heroes dare*
> *To die and leave their children free,*
> *Bid Time and Nature gently spare*
> *The shaft we raise to them and thee.*[52]

The news of the Battle of Lexington spread quickly and thousands of volunteer farmers from the surrounding colonies joined the Massachusetts militia. Within days this unorganized army besieged Boston. They were not strong enough to take the city but did hold Gage's troops at bay.[53]

Militiamen had come from all parts of New England to fight the British in Boston. On June 15th, the Americans held Breed's Hill. The British mounted three separate advances and were successful in forcing the Americans off the Hill in bitter hand-to-hand fighting. The victory for British forces was costly and, although the American siege on Boston was broken, both sides now realized that they had a bloody war on their hands.

Washington arrived too late to command the poorly organized American troops around Boston. General Gage had driven them from Breed's Hill in the Battle of Bunker Hill. In the meantime, while Gage's army was in control of Boston, American forces, led by Richard Montgomery and Benedict Arnold, won initial success against Canada; however, they were forced to retreat due to lack of support by the Canadian population for the rebellion.[54]

History has taught us that, if any war is justified, it was the revolution that America declared against England on July 6, 1775. For months after the war began, few Americans were willing to admit that independence was their primary intent; rather they sought individual and religious freedom. The revolutionary era fostered a favorable climate of ideas that powerfully reinforced the spirit of the Enlightenment, with intense belief in their "natural rights," liberty being the most precious gift. The beliefs and feelings of many patriot leaders at the time were summed up in Thomas Paine's early *Common Sense* pamphlet:

> God planned the colonies to be the nucleus of a great American
> nation, eventually to cover the continent.[55]

Early in 1776, the guns and supplies captured at Ticonderoga arrived in Cambridge. In March, Washington's forces captured and fortified Dorchester Heights, south of Boston, which General William Howe, who replaced Gen. Horatio Gates, had neglected to occupy. There he constructed two forts that prevented the British from keeping ships in Boston Harbor. General Howe realized that he could not hold Boston and sailed to Halifax with his army and hundreds of people still loyal to Britain.[55]

After April 1775, British authority remained in effect only in Boston. The Congress had instructed the colonies to reconstitute themselves as autonomous states. By early Spring 1776, all colonies were designing provisional governments that justified separation based on natural law or the law of Providence. They now realized that their survival depended on being united and acting "in congress." Richard Henry Lee, delegate from Virginia, offered the resolution stating that the "united colonies area, and of right ought to be, free and independent states." His motion was debated, adopted, sent to committee for drafting, revised and the *Declaration of Independence* was subsequently approved on July 4, 1776.

Throughout the colonies the *Declaration of Independence* was received with unbounded enthusiasm, so wrote Mrs. Adams in a letter to John Adams:

> After hearing a good sermon I went to hear the Proclamation for Independence proclaimed on King Street. Colonel Crafts read from the balcony of the State House and when he ended the cry from the balcony was "God save our American States" and cheers rent the air. After dinner the King's Arms were taken down from the State House and every vestige of him from every place and burnt in King Street."
>
> And all the people shall say Amen.[56]

The day before, General Howe had landed the first of 32,000 redcoats and Hessians on Staten Island. Nevertheless, the *Declaration* was read in all colonies by joyful patriots. Bells were rung and cannons were fired in celebration of our most precious document and a momentous step in the history of human freedom, supported with "a firm reliance on the protection of Divine Providence."[57]

Within a few months, knowing the importance of New York, Howe landed about 30,000 troops across the bay from Manhattan. Washington, anticipating the next British move, had shifted his troops to Long Island, a strategic position there. A large fleet, however, supported Howe's forces that served as a blockade of the New York Harbor and forced Washington to move his raw militia to Brooklyn where they were dealt a crushing blow. After another skirmish at White Plains, where Americans lost nearly 3,000 men along with Fort Washington and Fort Lee, they took refuge in Pennsylvania, across the Delaware River. Fortunately, Howe was in no hurry to pursue Washington, but used time offering pardons to patriots who would remain obedient to the king.[58]

"I regret" statement proclaimed by Nathan Hale, is set forth in all school history books and exemplifies his patriotism and bravery and is reflective of the spirit and sacrificial commitment by Americans during their war for independence. Captain Nathan Hale had volunteered to serve as a spy behind enemy lines in New York on September 21st. He was caught, treated badly, and hanged. His last words on the scaffold were, "I only regret that I have but one life to give for my country."

Nancy Hale, whose great-great-grandfather was Nathan Hale's brother, writes of her ancestor:

> Hale is a symbol of all American men who fight and who die for us. He is a symbol because he was the first of our heroes in the first of our own wars. His letters were destroyed so that the rebels should not know they have a man who can die so firmly. All of our nation's heroes are great men who are great by their minds and by their deeds and by their careers. All except Hale. His special gift to his country, and to us who love that country, was the manner of his death.[59]

This was a bleak time for the colonies, but spirits were lifted when Washington won two victories over British troops on the New Jersey side of the Delaware. Washington's concern now related to loss of troops due to enlistments ending at the end of 1776. With 10 days remaining, he attacked a detachment of Hessians stationed at Trenton. On Christmas night, before the river could freeze he ferried about 2,300 men across the ice-filled Delaware in a driving storm of sleet. The town was stormed at dawn. The commander, a Hessian, was killed and his force of 1,000 men, were taken prisoner. Eight days later, Washington defeated three British regiments at Princeton and moved his troops for winter quarters at Morristown, NJ.[60]

In 1777, the British began a new offensive centered near New York. Lieutenant General Burgoyne was assigned to take 8,000 men by way of Lake Champlain and the Hudson River to go to Albany to serve under Howe's command. Lieutenant Colonel St. Leger would bring other forces from Canada by way of Lake Ontario and to advance across upper New York State. Howe was to send a detachment up the Hudson to cooperate with the other commanders. Rather than sending troops up the Hudson, Howe transported them to Chesapeake Bay to capture Philadelphia. This caused St Leger's mission to fail. When his men were stopped by General Nicholas Herkimer and German settlers of the Mohawk Valley, where a bloody battle took place, St Leger returned to Canada. Burgoyne was then left alone to conquer New York. He was able to take Ticonderoga but suffered terrible losses every mile of his advance by the Continental Army and the colonial militia. He was eventually defeated at Stillwater near Saratoga. He retreated to Saratoga, but was heavily surrounded by American forces where he surrendered his entire army.[61]

Now alone, Howe continued to carry on a successful campaign against Philadelphia and, in the attempt to defend the capital, Washington faced the British at Brandywine, where he suffered heavy losses and, again, was defeated at Germantown. Howe was now in control of Philadelphia as well as the Delaware River and Delaware Bay.

Washington and his ragged army went into winter quarters at Valley Forge where we have come to know they suffered the worst hardships of he entire war. But God works his ultimate plan in mysterious ways. Washington's victory at Saratoga proved to be the turning point of the Revolution. France was now willing to make an alliance with America, inasmuch as American independence was probable. A treaty of commerce would be prized by France as well as well as a treaty of alliance in a war with England along with the hope to recover lost territory in the Mississippi Valley. Two treaties were signed with France in 1778.[62]

In Spring 1778, Sir Henry Clinton replaced Howe with orders to relocate troops from Philadelphia to New York. Washington's attempt to stop the British troops at Monmouth failed due to disloyalty by General Charles Lee, who disregarded Washington's orders by retreating rather than advancing, the decision that allowed Clinton to reach New York safely.

With the loosening of British control, American frontiersmen resumed their westward expansion, but along the frontier they had to fight British troops, their Indian allies and settlers who were still loyal to Britain. In 1778, 150 Kentucky volunteers led by George Rogers Clark, seized a British post on the Mississippi River and a post at Vincennes on the Wabash River that were havens of refuge for Indians who were attacking frontier settlements

At the close of the war, Clark controlled a large part of the territory north of the Ohio River. There were significant sea battles as well as those waged on land. The Continental Congress had managed to build only a few small armed vessels that were no match against the mighty British navy. However, they were aided by 2,000 privately owned armed vessels commissioned by the Congress or individual states. The contribution of the brave privateers to the cause of the Revolution was outstanding and historic. The exploits of such naval captains as John Paul Jones and John Barry served to establish the traditions of the early American Navy.

Because of the large population loyal to Britain in the southern colonies, they shifted their major operations from the middle colonies to the south where they were initially successful. In December 1778, they captured Savannah which cut Georgia from the rest of the colonies. They took Charleston in May 1780. In August 1780, General Gates, now Commander of the Continental forces, suffered a crushing defeat at Camden, SC, that left the south with only guerrilla resistance. The British advance was finally stopped by mountaineers and backwoodsmen from frontier settlements in Tennessee and North Carolina at the Battle of King's Mountain in October 1780. Gates was replaced by Gen. Nathaniel Green, who prevented further advances by the British and forced them to abandon all their posts in the interior. Notable in history books is the battle at Cowpens where a wing of Green's army wiped out a British force under the leadership of Daniel Morgan.

The early months of 1781 marked another bleak period for the Continental Army. Benedict Arnold had become a traitor and the war was going badly. However, Marie Joseph Paul Yves Roche Gilbert du Motier, Marquis de Lafayette (Lafayette), in 1779, had gone to France and was successful in obtaining French help. The following spring a force of 5,500 men landed at Newport, RI, and, in 1781, a powerful French fleet arrived at the West Indies.

After defeating Green's forces at North Carolina in March 1781, he turned northward into Virginia to fortify Yorktown. There, the combined French and American forces carried out a surprise attack that served to bring the war to a close. A threat of attack on New York served to occupy General Clinton. A combined force of Americans and French under Washington and Gen. Jean Baptiste Donatien de Vimeur, comte de Rochambeau (Rochambeau) marched to Chesapeake Bay to embark for Yorktown. French men-of-war, under the command of the de Grasse, were waiting there and subsequently fought off a British squadron that tried to bring help for Cornwallis by sea. The combined French and American assault began in late September and, on October 19, 1781, Cornwallis was forced to surrender. The *Treaty of Paris* marked the formal end to the war and gave about everything Americans fought for during the previous eight years.[63]

Chapter 7

The Declaration of Independence, Our Constitution and *Bill of Rights*

When the Revolutionary War ended, the 13 states did not see the need to give their Congress the power previously wielded by Parliament. A government had been created, but it had no legal basis. A provisional government had been set up under the *Articles of Confederation* in 1777, which allowed each state to retain its sovereignty, freedom and independence. The Provisional Government had provided unity needed during the war, but it was not legal and state leaders now realized that a properly constituted central government was necessary for national unity. The Constitutional Congress passed laws, but had no power to enforce them. Our country came into being as 13 independent states, according to the *Declaration of Independence*, each with its own laws. After the war, the *Articles of Confederation* served as the law of the land until 1789, but it was not a lawmaking body and could not function without such power to raise taxes, coin money and enter into treaties.[64]

The period in America after 1783 has been portrayed as a "country in chaos." After 10 years of war, the colonists looked forward to freedom and peace. By 1786, there was such distress that people demanded something be done to create a stronger and more effective government. The primary cause of the unhappiness was money. Some states issued their own money in coins or paper and levied duties on imports from other states and foreign countries. Britain had put heavy duties on American ships, and Spain closed their ports in Spain and America leaving American ships at the mercy of Barbary pirates. Congress had no power to raise taxes, regulate business or place duties on imports. People faced poverty and starvation or imprisonment for failure to pay their debts. Almost all states suffered from the flood of paper money that had no value.[65]

A letter was circulated by George Washington to all state governors to encourage the adoption of a more powerful government. Alexander Hamilton agreed and demanded the calling of a new congress or convention to draft a constitution based on firmer principles. There was widespread fear that states would lose their autonomy, but a small group in Virginia convinced their state legislature to call a general convention at Annapolis to discuss taxation and commerce. It was poorly attended but the Annapolis attendees were urged by Hamilton to urge the Congress to set a convention in Philadelphia to propose amendments to the *Articles*.

A new convention was arranged to meet in Philadelphia in May 1787 that lasted until September. Fifty remarkable men met privately in Independence Hall to make improvements to the *Articles* and make a more workable government. Washington came from Virginia and was immediately chosen president of the convention. James Madison, also from Virginia, came with a plan that he had formulated. However, it soon became clear that what was required was a federal government stronger than any single colonial state. It was then concluded to discard the *Articles of Confederation* and write a completely new constitution that provided for three departments: legislative, executive and judicial. Representation would be greater in larger states than smaller ones. Congress would have the power to legislate on all matters of national concern with which states could not deal, including the power to tax, regulate interstate and foreign commerce and spend money for defense and the general welfare.[66]

The new *Constitution* became legal when it was approved by nine states on May 20, 1790, with the understanding that a *Bill of Rights* would be added. Under the new *Constitution*, states could name congressmen and electors, who then chose George Washington as president and John Adams as vice president.

The *Constitution* did not satisfy all the delegates but the document was a triumph of practical statesmanship and gave the nation a stronger government than they had been living under, and states still retained their autonomy. As noted, in the process of working out the division of powers between the government and the states there was continuing concern about the liberties of individual citizens. The *Constitution* had not guaranteed some important ones. This was a bone of contention in state conventions that were called to ratify the *Constitution*. Some states had already enacted rights in their local constitutions, so there were precedents that would guarantee rights to people throughout the new nation. There was agreement that those rights should be listed and spelled out. Many of those who had opposed ratification of the *Constitution* were eager to have another convention and those who favored ratification believed that adopting a *Bill of Rights* would be an effective way to end opposition to ratification. James Madison had a lifelong interest in theology and saws the importance of religion in a republican society, took the lead in providing one.[67]

A great majority of Jews who dwelt in America supported the Revolution and the American cause from so small a community. Almost 100 Jews were identified as soldiers in the revolutionary armies. When the Constitutional Convention met there was fear that Jews would be excluded from voting and holding office, but the *First Amendment* strengthened the foundation of the Republic by decreeing the separation of church and state. In federal law, Jews, the smallest of all recognizable minorities now had totally unrestricted freedom and equality in the United States.[68]

Clarence Carson noted the mass of material that had come in from the states during and after ratification that amounted to proposals for such amendments. Two-hundred-ten recommendations had been submitted from the various states designed to protect rights of the people with the understanding that they would be added to the *Constitution*. Madison sifted through the amendments that had been proposed by the various state ratifying conventions and concluded that human liberties were a far less concern than the desire to curb the power of the federal government. He then reduced the list to 19 of which 10 were finally ratified to become a part of the *Constitution*.[69]

The *Bill of Rights* was written and ratified based on resolutions and petitions from the States requesting such an addition to the *Constitution*. First and foremost, was the demand for a religious provision to prevent the government from establishing a national church, which was set forth in the opening sentence of the *First Amendment*. Paul Johnson noted that on September 24, 1789, the day after the amendment was approved, a resolution was passed calling for a day of national prayer and thanksgiving. This *Establishment Clause*, to which it is frequently referred, is more fully understood and appreciated when we read in the Resolution:

> We acknowledge with grateful hearts the many signal favors of almighty God, especially affording them an opportunity peacefully to establish a constitutional government for their safety and happiness.

Washington's reply, on approving the holiday, well remembered.

> It is the duty of all nations to acknowledge the providence of Almighty God, to obey His will, to be grateful for His mercy, to implore His protection and favor . . . that great and glorious Being who is the beneficent author of all the good that was, that is, that ever will be, that we may unite in rendering unto Him our sincere and humble thanks for His kind care and protection of the people.[70]

Chapter 8

Repeal of the Establishment Clause

It is important to understand that the men who approved the amendments believed that no constitution *could grant rights; rather, they believed that rights set forth in the Declaration* of Independence and the *Constitution* were natural ones, gifts from the Creator, implanted in the nature of things.

Clarence Carson provides a clarifying examination of the conception of natural rights as our Founding Fathers conceived them within a framework of natural law:

> God reveals Himself and His purposes through nature's structure, order, and laws. To learn these, man uses his reason to discover both the underlying laws and the principles governing them. If, as many had come to believe by the middle of the 18th century, man ids entitled by God to natural rights, then it is a duty to defend them in society. Man must live in accord with nature's laws, if he is to achieve just and constructive purposes on earth. Most Americans of this time would have said that God not only reveals Himself through nature which is discoverable by reason but also through Scripture. Both are binding upon man.[71]

After revisions were made they were approved on December 15, 1791. The *First Amendment*, considered to be the most important, headed the list. It prohibited legislative action in certain areas, giving citizens freedom of religion, assembly, speech, and press, and he right to petition. The next seven secure the rights of property, and guarantee the rights of defendants accused of crimes. The ninth protects rights not specifically enumerated. The tenth, reinforcing this, insists that the "powers not delegated to the United States by the *Constitution* nor prohibited by it to the states, are reserved to the states respectively, or to the people.[72]

The *Bill of Rights* is not a grant of rights to the American people; rather, they are a body of prohibitions and limitations on the government. While the government is prohibited from establishing any religion, it is prohibited from interfering with the free exercise of any religion. Our founding fathers believed that the support of religion was essential to the well-being of the country.[73]

Early America schools were considered extensions of the home and church. As late as 1960 daily devotions and *Bible* reading were required and teaching of moral values, set forth in the Judeo-Christian *Bible*, was an essential part of the school curriculum. Many credit the character of public, private and parochial schools before 1940 for the emergence of the generation we refer to as "the greatest generation." To protect religious liberty and to moderate religious passions at the same time they recognized that religious values require public acknowledgement, common defense and mutual respect. Nothing has happened in the past two centuries to suggest that Washington, James Madison, John Adams, and Jefferson were wrong. They all envisioned a government as neutral, especially in religion, but sympathetic to religion, in general. Many of the men who founded America came to escape religious persecution and when the *Constitution*'s *Bill of Rights* was drafted their goal was to make sure all Americans maintained their right to practice their faith free from government interference with no federal favoritism to a particular creed. Madison believed and wrote that belief in God was "essential to the moral order of the world."[74]

The culture war now raging in America (Chapter 10) sets forth consequences of the deliberate misinterpretation of the First Amendment and is serving to remove every vestige of Judeo-Christian values, character and traditions in America. The belief here is that the Constitution and the Bill of Rights are straightforward, easily understood and mean exactly what is stated. The contrary school of thought is that it is a "living" document to be interpreted in light of changing times and conditions. We have seen a steady progression by the Federal judiciary since the period of the Warren Court to impose an interpretation of the First Amendment directly contrary to its guarantee.[75]

The *First Amendment* was most important to the colonists and to the state representatives who ratified the *Bill of Rights*. Numerous religions denominations were flourishing at the time. There was fear of a government that could possibly declare a national religion under the existing *Constitution*, but there was no thought that religion should be barred from government or the public square. The *Establishment Clause*, as we know it, prevented such action and guaranteed freedom to exercise religious belief in speech and action

Everson v. the Board of Education

There was little government interference in religion for the first 150 years of the American Republic, until 1947, when the Supreme Court considered the case styled *Everson v. the Board of Education*. The New Jersey law allowed use of public funds to bus pupils to parochial schools for religious instruction and the Board of Education reimbursed parents for children's fares. In *Everson*, the Court presented the strangest argument ever offered up to that time. A Ewing township taxpayer brought suit alleging that the New Jersey statute violated the *Establishment Clause*.

Until around the middle of the 19th century, the Supreme Court assumed that the *Bill of Rights* meant what it said—no more, no less—and legislative acts believed to be contrary to the *Constitution* were nullified. After 1930, however, the Supreme Court, under the influence of President Franklin Deleano Roosevelt and the New Deal, began to apply the *First Amendment* to state and local governments. *Lovell v. Griffin* in 1938 and *Cantwell v. Connecticut* in 1940 were early examples. Both cases had to do with freedom of speech. In 1960, the Warren court began making rulings about *Bible* reading in public schools which began efforts to drive religion out of public life and remove our government as defender of public morals. In 1962, the Court ruled on *Engel v. Vitale* against a prayer used in schools in New York that referred to "Blessings of Almighty God."[76]

It may serve a useful purpose at this point to recall Ed Meese's warning:

> The American people will never be able to regain democratic self-government—and thus shape public policy—until we curb activist judges who consider the *Constitution* a document of broad principles and concepts that empower them to substitute their personal beliefs, values, and policies for those enumerated in the *Constitution*.

This is in marked contrast to judges known as "originalists," who consider the text of the *Constitution* and the intent of the Founding Fathers when deciding a constitutional question, and believe they are obligated by it.

As noted before, government interference in religion was not serious for the first 150 years of the American republic until 1947, when the Supreme Court considered *Everson*. In this case, the Court presented the strangest argument ever offered up to that time. The New Jersey law allowed use of public funds to bus pupils to parochial schools for religious instruction. The Board of Education of the Ewing Township reimbursed parents for their children's fares. A Ewing Township taxpayer brought suit alleging that the New Jersey statute violated the establishment clause.[77]

Although the Court disagreed with the plaintiff, Justice Hugo Black, who wrote the majority opinion, stated that the state cannot exclude any student because of their various faiths from receiving the benefits of public welfare legislation. While this affirmed fair treatment for religion in the public sphere, other portions of the majority opinion established the antireligious precedent that has done so much damage to religious freedom.

He further stated, quoting from Thomas Jefferson's letter to the Danville Baptist Church:

> The *First Amendment* has erected a wall between church and state that must be kept high and impregnable. We could not approve the slightest breach.

Jefferson's figure of speech, in this case, was taken out of context, giving meaning not possible to Jefferson. It is reported that Justice Black was a fan of Jefferson with keen interest in Jefferson's "Wall of Separation" statement, along with his distain for the Catholic Church.[78]

It is helpful to recall Jefferson's entire reply to the Baptists in Danbury on January 1, 1802:

> GENTLEMEN: The affectionate sentiments of esteem and approbation which you are so good as to express towards me, on behalf of the Danbury Baptist Association, give me the highest satisfaction. My duties dictate a faithful and zealous pursuit of the interests of my constituents, and in proportion as they are persuaded of my fidelity to those duties, the discharge of them becomes more and more pleasing.
>
> Believing with you that religion is a matter which lies solely between man and his God, that he owes account to none other for his faith or his worship, that the legislative powers reach actions only, and not opinions, I contemplate with solemn reverence that

act of the whole American people which declared that the legislature should "make no law respecting an establishment of religion, or prohibiting the free exercise thereof," thus building a wall of separation between church and State. Adhering to this expression of the supreme will of the nation in behalf of the rights of conscience, I shall see with sincere satisfaction the progress of those sentiments which tend to restore to man all his natural rights, convinced he has no natural right in opposition to his social duties.

I reciprocate your kind prayers for the protection and blessing of the common Father and Creator of man, and tender you for yourselves and your religious association, assurances of my high respect and esteem.

The root of the controversy relative to the fallacious misinterpretation of the *Establishment Clause* has been widely and frequently documented. Recently, Mark Levin reminded of the letter that Jefferson wrote to a Baptist community in Danbury, CT. They had written a letter to Jefferson congratulating him on his election as president, and requested clarification regarding the *First Amendment* for religious dissenters, such as the Danbury Baptists, who were currently required to pay taxes to the established church in Connecticut.[79]

Newt Gingrich credits Michael Novak's report that Justice Black used an obscure letter written in 1802 referenced in *Reynolds v. United States,* heard in 1879, that involved a mistake in the transcription of Jefferson's original letter. Apparently the focus of *Reynolds* was not on "separation" but on the term "legislative powers" (which the translator had written), instead of Jefferson's original phrase, "legitimate power."[80]

In stating the issue, Justice Black misquoted the *First Amendment* three times in the same misquotation, in vogue today by those who seek to twist the *First Amendment* to mean something it clearly did not mean to its authors. The result was to give priority over the language of the *Constitution*. The question the court should have considered was what Madison meant by "establishment of religion" as opposed to "established religion." Justice Black and the concurring justices apparently had not read passages from *Annals of Congress,* or *The Separation of Church and State in Virginia* by Eckenrode. The complete separation of church and state had not been recognized by a president or Supreme Court from 1789 to 1948. In *Everson,* the Court set forth a new beginning with regard to the meaning of the *First Amendment,* a new beginning that wiped out the work of Jefferson, Madison, the Congress, the Presidency and the Supreme Court up to that date. Rather than guarantee religious freedom, it now means freedom from religion.[81]

In a review of books by Stephen Breyer, *Active Liberty: Interpreting our Democratic Constitution*, and Jonathan G. O'Neill's, *Originalism in American Law and Politics: A Constitutional History,* Michel M. Uhlmann traces the path to current judicial innovation and its consequences. O'Neill, Uhlmann states, gives strong support to the originalists' critique of judicial supremacy and the conception of the *Constitution* that is said to support it.[82]

Uhlmann has less praise for Breyer's contention that judges have a special obligation to rise above the framers' *Constitution* and the expressed will of elected lawmakers. He takes particular issue with Breyer's agreement with modern suppositions about the *First Amendment* in *Everson*.

Uhlmann correctly documents three things *Everson* did:

1. It applied the *Establishment Clause* against the states for the first time. (Heretofore, religion was left up to the states).
2. The *Everson* ruling read into the *Establishment Clause* Jefferson's metaphor concerning the "wall of separation" and altered and expanded the fundamental meaning of the amendment.
3. It made the Supreme Court the final arbiter of all matters regarding the relationship of government and religion.[83]

O'Neill believes that the source of "legal realism," seen in court rulings today, can be traced to Supreme Court Justice Oliver Wendell Holmes, Jr. Justice Holmes' mission was to separate legal thought from moral principles. Conception of objective moral principles, natural law and natural rights, (the bedrock of our *Constitution* and *Bill of Rights*), carries no legal authority. (Today, this is considered judicial activism.) American constitutionalism, deeply planted in the natural law tradition, attained its power by the end of the Enlightenment period, but its foundations were undermined during the 19th century. Socialism had begun to spread during Holmes' tenure on the Supreme Court but could not have been a factor in ideas and movements unless our *Constitution* were "changed, evaded or submerged."

Justice Black's opinion that undercut the true meaning of the religious clause drew widespread criticism in 1947 and is criticized widely today (as exemplified, in 2006, by Justice Black's induction into the Alabama State Bar Association's Hall of Fame). Tom Parker, Chief Justice of the Alabama Supreme Court, issued a statement that Black's induction is a "shameful disgrace to the people and State of Alabama." Chief Justice Parker said that Black personally launched the war to kick God out of the public square in America.[84]

How valid were the views of Chief Justice William H. Rehnquist in 1985 in his dissent in *Wallace v. Jaffree,* when he declared:

> The well accepted meaning of the *Establishment Clause* is that it merely prohibited the "establishment" of a national religion, that is, the designation of a national church. The *Establishment Clause* did not require governmental neutrality between religion, nor prohibit the government from providing non-discriminatory aid to religion. More, how valid is his belief regarding the meaning of Jefferson's letter to the Danville Baptists in his frequently quoted *Declaration.*[85]

The off-quoted metaphor statement proclaimed by the late Chief Justice William Rehnquist rings increasingly bold and sharp over the years. We pray that our Supreme Court will heed his warning.

> The wall of separation between church and state is a metaphor based on bad history, a metaphor which has proved useless as a guide to judging. It should be frankly and explicitly abandoned.

Americans for the Separation of Church and State (AU) acknowledge that a "lot of influential people in high places; the federal courts, the Congress, the state legislatures, and the White House, want to knock down the time-tested wall of separation between church and state." The AU also believes that "Rehnquist and company" are wrong as it protects freedom of conscience and has given Americans more religious freedom than any people in world history. They are fighting to keep it that way by speaking up for the "wall" in courts, in the halls of government and in the area of public opinion.[86]

Not until the *Establishment Clause* was formulated has it now being used to silence the American people. Opponents do not want religion in the public square and do realize that religion is the reason for the public square.

McCollum v. the Board of Education

Our Supreme Court considered the *McCollum v. the Board of Education* case a year later. The Illinois School Board, under state law, allowed a voluntary association of Jewish, Roman Catholic and Protestant faiths to conduct religion classes in school buildings during school hours. An atheist parent brought suit to end the practice after a year of participation by 800 satisfied students. The Illinois Courts upheld the practice, but the case was appealed to the Supreme Court of the United States.

The Supreme Court, as in *Everson*, which was supported by the American Civil Liberties Union (ACLU), completely disregarded history and true meaning of the *Establishment Clause*. Their discussion did not include the facts of history that could have set forth the intent of the *First Amendment*. Instead, the Justices discussed the language of Jefferson's figure of speech, "wall of separation." Justice Black's majority opinion dealt with the use of tax funds for religious instruction, which heretofore was legal. Also, as in *Everson*, the correct use of "establishment", and "established," was inconsistent with Justice Black's position.

Henry Pitney Van Dusen sounded a warning soon after *McCollum* in his book, *God in Education*, his effort not just to set forth the truth, but the important truth. He believed that religious instruction in schools was in serious question because of this case. He was so right. He made reference to the opinions of Edward S. Corbin of Princeton University who at the time was one of the most eminent authorities on the history and meaning of constitutional law. Professor Corbin held that the findings in *McCollum* were in error and offered the following summary:

1. The Court's intervention was most insubstantial.
2. The decision was based on a "figure of speech."
3. The decision is seen to stem from an unhistorical conception of what is meant by an "established religion."
4. The prohibition on the establishment of religion by Congress does not convert to a similar prohibition on the States, under the authorization of the *Fourteenth Amendment*.[87]

It would be difficult to adequately summarize the attitude and intent of the Founding Fathers along with the practice of the American nation regarding the role of religion in the heart of America since 1897. The State and religion, even the State and Church, had been intimately intermingled at all levels and in a variety of ways until the middle of the 20th century. They fully expected government to advocate public policy consistent with their religious beliefs.[88]

Chapter 9

One Nation Under God

America has been a Christian nation from its beginning. While there were numerous Protestant denominations, Catholics and Jews, they shared many common beliefs and forms of worship. In 1776, 98% of Americans professed to Protestant Christians, 1.8% professed to be Catholic and .2% said they were Jewish. Such a religious population should explain the progress of our nation from Jamestown to Philadelphia when our *Declaration of Independence*, *Constitution* and *Bill of Rights* were ratified.

In 1892, our Supreme Court examined the question of America as being a Christian nation, and after a review of hundreds of historical documents relative to the foundation of our nation, concluded in the Trinity Decision that such references add a volume of unofficial declarations to the mass of utterances that this is a Christian Nation. Such utterances are frequently proclaimed by latter-day patriots as John Whitehead:

> In seeking independence from Great Britain, the colonists declared to the world their belief in a personal infinite God—"their creator"—who endowed them with "certain inalienable" or absolute rights.
>
> To the men of that time, it was self-evident that if there were no God, there could be no absolute rights. Unlike the French revolutionaries a few years later, the American colonists knew very well that if the inalienable rights they were urging were not seen in the context of Judeo-Christian theism, they were without content.
>
> The *Declaration of Independence* therefore, is structured upon a Judeo-Christian base in two fundamental ways. First, it professes faith in a "Creator" who works in and governs the affairs of men in

> establishing absolute standards to which men re held accountable. Second—and even more fundamentally, since all Western nations of that era professed a belief in the Creator—there is the idea that man is a fallen creature and hence, cannot be his own law-giver and judge. In the end, it is God to whom the appeal must be made. In this sense, the law cannot be simply what a judge or a fuehrer says it is. It is what God says it is.[89]

By the middle of the 18th century the influence of the Puritan ethic had greatly diminished, but as earlier noted the Christian movement it set in motion was firmly established. The hand of God seemed to be continually shaping America. The Puritan belief that government and religion were inseparable was seen in the continuing election of revolutionary leaders whose actions reflected this belief. Research of private correspondence left behind by the founding fathers shows overwhelming evidence of their belief in the importance of God and Christianity in public life. A number of patriotic historians have chronicled a panorama that over the years have reinforced the character of our nation.[90]

Clarence Carson described the foundations of American Constitutionalism, and our *Constitution*, as philosophical, historical, traditional, rationalistic and carried a substrata of religious sanctions. The founders believed man was made in the image of God, forged from Divine Fire, God breathed life into him, and that He is rightly to be called Father. They drew on this substrata of religious belief in believing that man's being virtuous, honorable, and trustworthy informed their belief of the possibility of liberty and self-government. Our ordered universe, created by God, is essential for liberty; otherwise chaos will result, along with massive government to maintain order.[91]

Symbols of our nation's faith are still displayed in public and private buildings throughout our country, but in agreement with Senator Robert Byrd:

> There is no other place in the United States are there so many, and varied official evidences of deep and abiding faith in God on the part of governments as there are in Washington.

It is an uplifting experience to view such precious documents first-hand in our National Archives. Dr Dave Miller, in his discourse, *America, Christianity and the Culture War,* has conveniently listed such displays by specific categories:

Statements and Actions of Belief

The Second Virginia Convention in 1775, a year before the signing of the *Declaration of Independence*, was held in a church building. Patrick Henry, one of the great founders, was in attendance. It was on this occasion that he gave his memorable, "Give me liberty or death," speech. He spoke of responsibility to God, Majesty of Heaven, which he revered above all earthly kings, God of Hosts, the God of Nature who presides over the destinies of nations to help in our battles. His frequent appeals to God were typical of the Founders as they assigned a theological rationale for the Revolutionary War.

The Constitutional Convention, held in Philadelphia in 1787, was called to hammer out political principles that were to guide the new Nation. The assembly had stalemated due to strife and disagreement. Benjamin Franklin, who may have been labeled the least religious of the founders, made his majestic remarks that served to bring harmony to the assembly, and the subsequent formulation of our remarkable *Constitution*. His remarks were thoroughly saturated with allusions to God and the *Bible*. Not widely remembered is the occasion of Franklin's attendance at a religious revival at which the revivalist George Whitefield preached. Franklin empted his pockets when the collection plate was passed.

The National Archives contains the original *Declaration of Independence*, the document with the immortal phrase declaring that, "we are endowed by the Creator with certain unalienable rights among which are life, liberty, and the pursuit of happiness."

The National Archives contains an image of the *Ten Commandments*, the Judeo-Christian beliefs that formed the foundation of our laws.

On September 24, 1789, the House adopted its resolution to request the President recommend to the people of the United States, a day of public thanksgiving prayer to acknowledge the many signal favors of Almighty God, especially for affording them the opportunity to establish a constitution of government for their safety and happiness.

On January 7, 1792, a Congressional Committee, with James Madison as member, was authorized to plan the chaplain system for Congress. It was implemented the following day. Congress has convened by prayer and worship continually to this present day.

In his reflections on the origins of our Nation, John Quincy Adams, the sixth president of the United States, stated his belief that from the days of the Revolution, the people of the North American Union and its constitutional states were associate bodies of civilized men and Christians, bound by the laws of God and the Gospel. When the shackles of British dependency were removed, the United States of America became an independent nation of Christians.

Noah Webster is known for his work to standardize American English but should also be remembered for the underpinnings of American government. His view that religion under a free government should be taught to all children and the Christian religion should be the basis of any government of a free people.

Elias Bandinot, who served as President of the Continental Congress, at the First Provincial Congress in New Jersey in 1782, reminded his fellows that "We are Christians, and the eyes of the world are now turned. Let us call on Christ to preside in our councils."

In April 1955, a Congressional prayer room, approved by the 83rd Congress, was in use. Legislators now had a cloistered retreat to pray and meditate about weighty issue they faced. Inspirational lift is centered in the stained glass window of George Washington kneeling in prayer, behind which is etched, Psalm 16:1: "Preserve Me, O God, for in Thee do I put my trust."

Religion and the Courts

The Founding Fathers, had they been living, would have been gratified with the judicial system that they had established, and the affiliation with the true God and the one true religion.

In 1810, the New York State Supreme Court found a man guilty of "scandalous, malicious, wicked and blasphemous speech in contempt of the Christian religion and the laws of the state". The conviction was upheld. To revile, with malicious and blasphemous contempt was an abuse of his right of the religion professed by almost the whole community.

In 1824, the Supreme Court of Pennsylvania declared America's unflinching attachment to the general precepts of the Christian religion in that "Christianity is part of the common law of this state."

In 1799, the Supreme Court of Maryland was unanimous in ruling that, "By our form of government, the Christian religion is the established religion."

In 1892, the United States Supreme Court cited instance after instance, proof after proof, that from the very beginning, America was aligned with the God of the *Bible*.

Our Currency

Salmon P. Chase, Secretary of the Treasury in 1861 under Abraham Lincoln, said, "No nation can be strong except in the strength of God, or safe except in His defense. The trust of our people should be declared on our national coins." Three years later, an Act of Congress approved the motto, "In God We Trust" to be placed on American coins beginning with the two-cent piece in 1864.

National Symbols

The story of the Liberty Bell and that is cracked at the first announcement of the *Declaration of Independence* is well-known to most school children. Not so well-known to them is that the inscription encircling the bell is taken from Leviticus 25:10, "Proclaim liberty throughout the land unto all the inhabitants thereof." The same Biblical verse is inscribed on the Statue of Liberty on Bedloe's Island in New York Harbor.

Our national seal, authorized by the Continental Congress on July 4, 1776, was an effort to embody the beliefs and values the Founding Fathers wanted to pass on to their descendents. The design selected by Benjamin Franklin, John Adams and Thomas Jefferson depicted Moses crossing the Red Sea with Pharaoh in hot pursuit with the motto, "Rebellion to tyrants is obedience to God."

Architecture

References to God are prominent in government buildings in Washington, DC, and state capitals and other government buildings throughout our country. Our Supreme Court contains several allusions to the *Ten Commandments*. The Library of Congress includes eight statues representing life and thought. The one labeled "History" is engraved with Lord Tennyson's words, "One God, One Law, One element and one far-off divine event, to which the whole creation moves." The verse from Mica 6:8, is engraved on the statue of Religion. Above the figure of science are the words from Psalm 19:1: "The heavens declare the glory of God and the firmament showeth His handiwork."

Statues of Paul and Moses can be seen along the balustrade of the galleries and among the murals in the dome of the main reading room are the words: "Thou shalt love thy neighbor as thyself."

The Adams Prayer Mantel in the White House, which dates back to 1800, is the inscription that appeals to God: "I pray Heaven to bestow the best of blessings on this house and all that shall hereafter inhabit it." Images of the *Ten Commandments* are seen in a statue in front of the Ronald Reagan Building titled: "Liberty of Worship."

In the House Chamber of the United States Capital complex, are the words, "In God We Trust" engraved in marble on the wall behind the Speaker of the House. A stained glass window showing George Washington praying on one knee is in the chapel of the U.S. capital with the inscription from Psalm 16:1, along with the words: "This Nation under God."

The Lincoln Memorial houses references to some of Lincoln's speeches that are punctuated with references to God and the *Bible*, along with an inscription of the *Gettysburg Address* in which he proclaims, "This Nation under God."

Numerous references to God are seen in the Jefferson Memorial such as "I have sworn upon the Alter of God," "A mighty God hath created the mind free," "God who gave us life gave us liberty," and "God is just, that His justice cannot sleep forever."

The apex of the Washington Memorial is topped by an aluminum capstone with the Latin words: "*Laus Deo* (Praise be to God)." The internal stairway of the Washington Monument contains stones that abound with references to God, the *Bible* and Christian morality.

The occasion of the inauguration of Washington as our first president should remind and affirm the belief of America as a Christian nation and its religious heritage. Bruce and William Catton describe the brief but moving event that took place on April 30, 1789 at Federal Hall:

> The portico contained a single chair and a table draped in red, topped by a *Bible* resting on a velvet cushion. Washington seated himself momentarily while the appointed dignitaries—Vice President Adams, Governor Clinton, New York's Chancellor Robert Livingston, Generals Knox and St. Clair, and a few others—took their places on the portico. Washington rose to face Livingston, who stepped forward to administer the oath.
>
> Samuel Otis held the *Bible*. While Washington placed his hand on it, Livingston read the sonorous oath that every American Chief executive would hear and repeat at the outset of his term, and Washington became the first President . . . and . . . preserve, protect, and defend the *Constitution of the United States*.

"So help me God," Washington concluded, bending forward to kiss the *Bible*.[92]

No more appropriate concluding statement can serve to reaffirm a strong belief that America is indeed a Christian nation one that summarized such a list of our nation's faith in "The Rebirth of America.

> This nation, without reasonable doubt, was established on the firm foundation of scripture. Our forefathers, brilliant as they were, openly acknowledged the true genius behind the new system to be the eternal principles of God's Word. The most fundamental concepts of the republic find their roots in the *Bible*.
>
> From the beginning, the basis for law and government in American society was decidedly biblical. What's more, the new land was forged through the energy of the -Christian work ethic.
>
> The United States in her first century of existence knew the stinging reality of conflict. There were wars, assassinations, injustices catastrophes and plagues of disease. But the young nation endured, for its moral fabric had been woven with the durable threads of Scriptural truth. Societal ills, like slavery, were ultimately recognized for what they were: violations of God's standard.
>
> The record of the establishment of America bears the clear stamp of Christian influence. The impact of the Gospel is evident in the leaders chosen, the laws written, and the sweeping changes brought about through the transforming power of Christ in the individual lives and corporate experience. American was not formed a nation apart from God, but a nation under God.[93]

Chapter 10

America's Culture Wars

The suicidal attacks by Islamic terrorists in New York City and Washington, DC, on September 11, 2001, were, by their admission, an act of religious war motivated by their extreme religious beliefs. This sad date is now seared in the American conscience to be remembered for generations. The stated goal of the terrorists, not shared by Muslims who live by the tenets of the original Qu'ran, is to destroy Israel and America and convert the world to their abberrated extremist Islamic beliefs.

Unfortunately, America is presently involved in two wars. While the war with Islamic terrorists is somewhat recent, their goal is to destroy Israel and America and convert the world to Islam. The second, one that we call a culture war, has been going on for decades, but both are religious wars. The goal of the second has the objective of redefining the character of America and converting our nation to a secular one.

Our wars with terrorists and secularists are foreboding with no end in sight. We may have the will and means to confront terrorists on their terrain, but the war with terrorists and the "cultural" war in America, are now being waged within our borders. Martin Gross shouted an earlier warning about this danger. In 1997, he documented the failure of our government and pointed to internal weaknesses in American civilization and another phenomenon—a social and cultural madness that "distorts virtually everything we do or contemplate—is ravaging us internally, a force that he labeled; "The New Establishment." It has shaped a potent attack on the nation's mind and morale.[94]

Similar alarms have been sounded in publications and addresses by an increasing number of concerned, informed and responsible public figures, all sterling patriots, but their pleas may go unheeded without the force of legal action.

Michael Savage, pseudonym of Dr. Michael Alan Weiner, Ph.D. warned of this in his recent book, *The Enemy Within*. He sets the purpose and tone of this timely publication with the telling quote from Marcus Tullius Cicero, the distinguished Roman statesman:

> A nation can survive fools, and even the ambitious. But it cannot survive treason from within. An enemy at the gates is less formidable, for he is known and carries his banner openly. But, the traitor moves against those within the gates freely, his sly whispers rustling through all the alleys, heard in the very halls of government.[95]

Our present plight evokes memory of a story of a Trojan and Greek war set in mythology. The Trojans had taken refuge from Greek onslaughts behind the safety of their city walls. The desperate Greeks seized on Ulysses advice and build a great wooden horse with a secret door to hide some warriors. When the Greeks parked it outside the city wall, the Trojans saw the Greeks leave and believed they were now safe. They then hacked down an open space in the wall and moved the great horse inside. During the night the armed soldiers came from the horse and opened the city gates to allow waiting Greek soldiers to come in. After 10 long years of Greek attacks, the city was finally taken and left in ruins.

The conclusion that America is being redefined is not debatable. What we are becoming is not a nation that our forefathers envisioned, nor is it a world that our World War II Generation knew and are now "shaking their heads." Reasons for the culture war in America include such issues as abortion, homosexuality, Darwin's theory of organic evolution, gun control, school prayer, the *Ten Commandments*, pornography, English as our official language, same-sex marriage, and freedom of speech. All such issues may be included, but the root explanation is that we are in a life or death struggle over whether Jehovah, the Judeo-Christian God of the *Bible*, will continue to be the source of America's goodness and greatness.

Angelo Codevilla wrote that the role of government plays a role in engineering vast differences in civic, economic life, family customs and souls that separate our nation from the nation of our founders, is self-evident. One part of society has enlisted government in an effort to "shove an alien way of life down its throat." As early as 1930, no one could have conceived of

Supreme Court decisions that would take schools out of the hands of local citizens, religion out of public life, protect obscenity, establish abortion and protect other debilitating changes in American life. At stake is whether modern America will reassume the habits of America's founders. Our culture war is about two sets of separate and unequal beliefs and ways of life that is sorting out people who strive to live under the *Ten Commandments* in the face of those who live by an atheistic, secular religion.[96]

The atheistic secular movement made little headway before the middle of the twentieth century primarily due to a population imbued with traditional family values and courts that recognized and abided by the intent of our *Constitution*. The remarkable success achieved by the counterculture can only be explained by liberal judges who feel comfortable in ruling on precedents set forth in cases beginning with liberal Supreme Court rulings during the period that Earl Warren served as Chief Justice.

The attitude of the first congress relative to the intent of the *First Amendment's* clause on religion is clear. The American people believed that control over religion should be left in the hands of the states. This made it impossible for congress to establish a national church. This constitutional arrangement met its first defeat in the decision in *McCollum*.

In early campaigns to destroy the *First Amendment* there were no fewer than 11 separate formulations of amendments submitted between 1870 and 1888. All were repudiated by responsible and authoritative representatives of the American people. The unbroken record from 1789 to 1948 has been an emphatic refusal to accept the doctrine reflected in *Everson*.

Today, this doctrine has become a constitutional principle.

The *First Amendment* is now at the center of the culture war. Religion and Judeo-Christian values have been banished from public schools (the principle agency in shaping children and youth for citizenship in America), from public buildings and the public square. This is being done by using federal courts to circumvent the will of the people, and by promoting a deliberate misinterpretation of the meaning of the *First Amendment*. The counterculture organizations and numerous, but two most prominent, who use the courts to achieve their ends, are the ACLU and Americans United for the Separation of Church and State (AU)

The ACLU has a well-deserved reputation as a scourge of religion in the public square. Their mission statement says that they serve as guardian of our nation's liberty by defending and preserving individual rights guaranteed by our *Constitution* and laws.[97] It assumes to function to conserve America's original civic values, the *Constitution* and *Bill of Rights*. This organization was established by Roger Baldwin in 1917 as the "Bureau for Conscientious Objection of the American Union against Militarism," but later was changed to "Civil Liberties Bureau." In 1918 the FBI raided Baldwin's office to search for subversive materials. Baldwin then served a year in prison for sedition. In 1920, he founded the ACLU. Its present membership is reported to be 250,000 with 300 chapters nationwide, a legislative office in Washington, DC, and a powerful legal staff that handles about 6,000 cases annually in almost every state.[98]

While the ACLU claims to champion the cause of religious liberty it has done more harm than any other organization to eliminate Judeo-Christian influence in America based on *First Amendment* decisions in 1947 and 1948. J. M. O'Neill's career with the ACLU, as member for 12 years and four as Chairman of its committee on Academic Affairs, made him:

> . . . increasingly aware of the tremendous misunderstanding and confusion throughout the whole field of civic liberties, especially in regard to the purpose and effect of the *Bill of Rights.*

In his landmark book, *Religion and Education under the Constitution*, written during the time of *Everson* and *McCollum*, Dr. O'Neill predicted:

> Unless the American people stop the current trend, and force a return to the doctrines of democratic decision and of the *Constitution* as written and ratified by the American people, we shall drift inevitably into a regimented society under the unrestrained dictatorship of the men on the Supreme Court.[99]

Mark Levin, in relating observed motives of the ACLU, points out that judges are now the tool by which this organization pursues its obsession against displays of the *Ten Commandments* on public property. The ACLU has filed so many suits against such displays that it would take a separate page on its website devoted to them. Its legal victories or pending cases against the *Ten Commandments* stretch the length and breadth of our land, from Montana to Georgia, from California to Kentucky. He points out that the ACLU is not alone in this movement. The AU has filed similar actions.[100] The AU was founded in 1947 and purports to work on a wide range of pressing political and social issues. The AU boasts that it has led the way in defending the separation of church and state. In January 2002, the AU's powerful publication, *Church and State*, included an article titled, *Priority Mail*, which underscored the erroneous and misguided interpretation of Jefferson's letter to the Danbury

Baptist Church. The article includes a quotation of belief by Prof. Robert M. O'Neil, who teaches church-state law at the University of Virginia in which he proclaims his misguided belief, "we have always been and will remain a secular state."[101]

Two great wooden horses are parked within American walls today.

Chapter 11

Our Public Schools—A Melting Pot No More

The origin of the "melting pot" to describe America may not be actually known, along with what it is intended to mean. Over generations it has been used to describe a process of assimilation of a variety of immigrant cultures into one unique, specific culture. The "melting pot" figure of speech is used in school history books to describe New Netherlands 1624, which became a melting pot of people from various nations. Fifty years later, 16 languages could be heard on the streets of New Amsterdam. Herbert George (H. G.) Wells, in his 1916 book, *Mr. Britling Sees It Through*, he described America as the "New World, where there are no races and nations anymore. She is the melting pot from which we will cast the better state."[102] The English author, Israel Zangwill, Jewish man of letters, also popularized the figure of speech. All European cultures, he stated in his 1908 play *The Melting Pot*, would be blended and from them a novel and superior culture would emerge.[103]

It is telling that early life on the frontier settlements where various religious denominations, social position did not matter. Most immigrants abandoned their various cultures and adapted Anglo characteristics with English as the dominant language. Nearly all white settlers—Protestants, Catholics and Jews, were deeply religious. Each had its own doctrines and forms of worship, but with common beliefs. This Judeo-Christian tradition was a powerful force in uniting our nation into what we enjoy calling, "The American Way," embodied with the two most precious human yearnings—individual freedom and religious freedom, both reflected in early American history, our *Constitution* and *Bill of Rights*.

Throughout the period of colonial settlements, from Jamestown, landing of the Puritans, to New England and the Great Awakenings, parents wanted their children to learn to read, primarily to read the *Bible*. Parents assumed this responsibility first, later in parish churches, neighborhood schools, and then academies. Colleges were soon established by several sects, primarily to prepare young men for the ministry; the first, Harvard in 1636, followed by William and Mary in 1693. Six others were established before the Revolution.[104]

Benjamin Franklin said in his 1749 book, *Proposal Relating to the Education of Youth*, "Religious toleration could best be achieved to treat religion as one of the main subjects in school and relate it to character training." Alexis De Tocqueville also noted that "Religion was the underpinning of republican government. It was education that made the spirit of independence possible."[105]

From 1700 to the 1870's, Americans had considered the urgent need for an educational system to replace those of the colonial era. As they set up a republican form of government dedicated to equality, democracy, and freedom, they realized the need for an educational system to ensure such a form of government. A range of languages were still spoken, people held on to different cultures with no tradition of self-government, and some were proud or jealous of rule by others.

The American system of public education, with compulsory attendance, is the oldest in the world, traced back to the Act passed by the Massachusetts Bay Colony in 1647. We know it as the famous, *Ould Deluder Satan Law*, which early provided for public funding. None should deny that over generations our public schools can rightly be considered as the crucible for the American "melting pot" and have made democracy work. They have met high expectations to prepare children and youth for responsible citizenship. This goal has been unchanging and fits snugly in a framework of four educational objectives that provide for:

- National security
- Intellectual development
- Perpetuation of our unique culture
- Citizenship in American representative democracy

Religious sentiment in the Colonies was basic and the dynamic motive from the time that children were taught at home, through the Puritan era and followed by tax supported schools that began as a result of the 1642 Act by the Massachusetts Bay Colony. Education during the colonial era might be likened to a period of gestation leading to the birth of our Nation in 1776. From the beginning, concern about different religions was considered and religious doctrines common to all religions with non-secular principles contained in the *Bible*. Our schools nourished and shaped a heritage that resulted in our unique *Declaration of Independence*, *Constitution* and *Bill of Rights*, and the framework for the realization of mans' long search for individual freedom and religious freedom.

Philosopher-historian R. Freeman Butts expressed his concern for the future of the public schools, and our nation, in 1977:

> Until almost yesterday the public school was a fixed article of faith in the American public creed, commanding powerful moral authority as a national unifier, liberator, and equalizer. For a long time public education has a persuasive moral as well as legal authority behind it. At various times in the past the public school has drawn upon the political authority of the founders of the Republic, the religious authority of nondenominational Protestantism, the work ethic of middle class virtues, the academic authority of literacy and knowledge in an education-oriented society, the cohesive authority of assimilator and Americanizer in an immigrant-flooded society, and the socializing authority as agent of progressive reform in a rapidly modernizing and industrial society.[106]

Butts moved to express concern that the erosion of the legitimacy of some of the major institutions in American society has begun to effect "deauthorization" of the public schools as well, that is, "its moral authority to act as a guide or leader in social affairs and is seriously questioned."

It is no surprise that organizations that promote a false understanding of the *Establishment Clause* have, and continue to target our public schools to achieve their misguided agenda. After their early successes in *Everson* and *McCollum,* the president then set has been continuously followed in liberal courts and judges throughout our Nation. A frog, being cooked in warm water, finds that it is too late to hop out when the water boils. Similarly, our apathetic Nation heard the "alarm bells" in 1962 with the news of *Engle v. Vitale* that outlawed prayer in schools. Hopefully, our nation is now waking up.

Ironically in *Church and State*, the house organ for AU, there is a brash proclamation that public schools are under assault by the "radical" Religious Right and its allies. The Religious Right's allegation states that schools are now teaching humanism and other anti-God ideas. They acknowledge the "mess of prayer in schools", and say, "With the Religious Right—and some courts—touting student-led religious worship at public school events, does Church-State Separation have a prayer?[107]

Our public schools have served well to achieve educational goals as well as the primary agency in shaping and maintaining a unified, socially cohesive nation. Generations of immigrants have merged their varied backgrounds into a naturalization process that has assimilated customs, language, ideals, and values into a society that we characterize as the "American Way." We take pride in the role of our schools to make this possible. Over the past 200 years, the American society has been marked by extensive change and, of all social institutions that have responded to the evolving demands and expectations of each successive generation, it has been our schools that have discharged their obligations with amazing success.

Our public schools cannot ignore God. To ignore Him is to deny Him. Atheists may teach their children that there is no God and our schools must respect their rights, but atheists cannot require schools to teach atheism, otherwise, the *Declaration of Independence* and our historic traditions are based upon a fallacy.[108]

How far we have come since 1789 is exemplified in the recent action of the Michigan State Board of Education. The influence of the Michigan State governor, who believes that Evolution needs to be taught in science classes and not include Intelligent Design, apparently influenced the Board to approve such a curriculum guideline. Intelligent Design has become an issue in the race for governor in the forthcoming election.

The ACLU was concerned that "State standards would not be strong enough to prevent inclusion of Intelligent Design as the science course was written this summer."[109]

It is contended here that anyone with "walking around sense" must know in his heart and spirit that Darwinian evolution is ridiculous and is not scientifically untested, as one Board member stated. In contrast, as contended here, Intelligent Design is confirmed by voluminous studies based on sound documentation set forth in responsible scientific studies.

The process of shaping and nourishing our national character in keeping with the tenants of Judaism and Christianity seems to have ceased and we no longer "walk with God" as God told Abraham.

Our Public Schools—A Melting Pot No More.

Chapter 12

Reclaiming America

The history of the world, as noted before, is a history of religion, and is readily seen in the strand woven into the historical fabric of America from its beginning to the present time. De Tocqueville observed that religion was the first of American political institutions, a kind of Judeo-Christianity. He wrote:

> Religion filled every nook and cranny of the public square and the regime's tone because both political and ecclesiastic authority exercised by, of, and for a *Bible*-toting people.

De Tocqueville's belief about a "*Bible*-toting people," is seen in another of his continuing statements relative to religion in America. When he listed principle causes for the first political institution, he said that he had no doubt that the great severity of American mores was due primarily to religion.[110]

Americans, in recent years, have adopted laws, customs and habits that are in sharp contrast to what our founding fathers intended. Our government has become one of the main weapons for those who seek to denigrate and diminish the role of religion and has effectively driven it out of our public schools and public places.

The issue of "Church and State" was a continuous concern throughout our early history, to reach a conclusion only after the *Establishment Clause* was ratified. The colonists simply did not want a State church, or religious persecution, from which they were now free. Also, they now had freedom of speech, a component of the *Establishment Clause*, which they wanted to be guaranteed.

As a keystone, removed from its setting at the top of a sturdy archway causes the stonework to crumble, so has the series of Supreme Court rulings established precedents that serve to redefine the character of America. *Everson v. the Board of Education*, the first successful ACLU case, and the series of cases that quickly followed, provided "a baseball bat to beat Christianity into submission."

Unfortunately, the "loudspeaker" has been in the hands of the popular media. The drift away from our allegiance to traditional principles and values was not a sudden development, and charting and embarking on a new course will not be easy or sudden, but must be achieved through our courts, as the secularists did to achieve theirs.

Mark Levin strongly supports a belief, frequently stated in previous chapters, that our Supreme Court is abusing its constitutional role and has chosen to become the unelected, unassailable social engineer of American society. Sadly, he adds, other branches of government are complicit in the Court's power grab. He quotes Edwin Meese, former Attorney General of the United States under President Ronald Reagan, who described our constitution as "the most wonderful work ever struck off at a given time by the brain and purpose of man." He cautions, however, that it can fulfill that purpose only if it faithfully interpreted by those responsible for its application to our legal system.[111]

Two most egregious offenses of this warning, frequently noted in this book, were demonstrated in 1947 in *Everson* and *McCollum*. Arguably, the rulings in the two Supreme Court cases could cause our nation to suffer the fate suffered by Sodom and Gomorrah The view of America today, also previously noted, is characterized by forces of Humanism (Gnosticism), atheism, Darwinism, social liberalism, multiculturalism and political correctness. All have gradually succeeded in dismantling many of the moral and spiritual principles that were once considered the bedrock of American society. The religious and law-abiding segment of America, the backbone of our Nation, is bewildered and frustrated as they endure the disintegration of our moral and spiritual underpinnings.[112]

As hunters lost in the woods know they must find their way back to the place where they took a wrong turn, America must do the same. Organizations such as the ACLU and AU, failed to reshape America by removing religion from government, public schools, and the public square. Failing to influence the people directly, they focused their tactics through judicial action and liberal judges who disregard our heritage, our *Constitution*, the *Bill of Rights*, and the unbroken judicial record from 1789 to 1947. The Supreme Court of the United States has been wrong before, but it has ways of correcting its own misreading of the law as well as of changing law whose established readings it feels to be obsolete.

The American people must demand that our *Constitution* be interpreted as its authors intended. The majority of our citizens want a society in which God is allowed and honored in churches, synagogues and mosques, as well as outside. Unfortunately the "loudspeaker" has been in the hands of much of the popular media.

The drift away from our allegiance to traditional principles and values was not a sudden development, and charting and embarking on a new course will not be easy or sudden, but must be achieved through our courts, as secularists did to achieve their dark objectives.

Mark Levin, the distinguished constitutional lawyer, author and talk show host, tells about dispirited and alarmed callers to his radio show to question why so many of our nations great issues are decided by the federal courts. He draws on his extensive knowledge and experience to address this very question in his compelling and enlightening book, *Men in Black*. He uses examples of ways to rid the courts of unelected and unassailable social engineers. Supreme Court justices, he contends, as well as appellate court judges, can be impeached and Congress has constitutional authority to change the methods by which judges are disciplined. More potent and practical would be the use of Congress's power to limit the jurisdiction. But, Levin cautions that the aforementioned strategies are not "systemic" solutions to judicial abuse; rather, their influence can be reduced with a constitutional amendment to limit their terms of office rather than for life terms as is now the practice.

The most effective step Congress could take, Levin, believes, would be a constitutional amendment limiting the court's judicial review power by establishing a legislative veto over court's decisions by a two-thirds vote of both houses. Until such a constitutional amendment might be approved, the promise of a judicial strategy was reported in the recent Fox News documentary, *Church and State*. Hosted by Brit Hume, he noted that, whereas previous litigation has been ruled based on the misunderstanding of the First amendment, recent cases have been ruled on "freedom of speech," and which bodes hope for Country.[113]

Brit Hume, ably and proudly, traced the history of our Nation from its Judeo-Christian roots to the present time, citing judicial rulings that have been used to silence our people. Our hope was rekindled when he cited a series of court cases, in which the American Center for Law and Justice prevailed, based not on church and state, but on freedom of speech. His striking summary harmonizes melodiously with the theme of this book, "Secularists do not want religion in the public square, but religion is the reason for the public square."[114]

Fortunately, we are still a nation of laws, and the burden of change will fall to the hands of enlightened voters. The *Rebirth of America*, a timeless collection of essays, published by the Arthur S. DeMoss Foundation, reflects God's hand in the development of America as a Christian nation from its establishment to the present time, the time that many writers refer to as a "nation adrift." The voice and power of the people is heard and seen when we exercise our rights as American citizens. Power can be generated to make a difference when citizens commit to carry out such duties as:

- Register to vote, and vote
- Become informed
- Contact your elected officials
- Support good candidates
- And always—pray.[115]

So Mote it Be.

Endnotes

1. Gavian, Ruth Wood & William A. Hamm, *United States History* (D.C. Heath & Company,. 1960), p. 3.
2. Gavian & Hamm, p. 3.
3. Copeland, Lewis. *High School Subjects* (Halcyon House, 1943) p. 45.
4. Gavian & Hamm, pp. 11-12.
5. Gavian & Hamm, p. 125.
6. Taylor, Alan, *American Colonies* (Viking Penguin, 2001), p. 33.
7. Angle, Paul M., *The American Reader* (Rand McNally & Company, 1958), p. 3.
8. Kennedy, D. James, *Remember Our Foundation* (Sermon, Fort Lauderdale Presbyterian Church, October, 8, 2006).
9. Taylor, p. 33.
10. Taylor, p 38.
11. Muzzey, David Saville, *Our Country's History* (Ginn & Company, 1957), p. 31.
12. Taylor, p. 31.
13. Johnson, Paul, *A History of the American People* (Harper Collins, 1947), pp. 4-9.
14. Eibling, Harold H., Frederick M. King, & James Harlow, *Our United States* (Laidlaw Brothers, 1961), p. 70.
15. Canfield, Leon & Howard B. Wilder, *The Making of Modern America* (Houghton Mifflin Company, 1964), pp. 50-55.
16. Gavian & Hamm, p. 30.
17. Gavian & Hamm, p. 27.
18. *Jamestown, World Book, Volume 10* (Educational Corporations, 1963), pp. 24-25.
19. Carson, Clarence B., *Basic American Government* (American Textbook Committee, 1993), p. 161.
20. Gavian & Hamm, p. 71.
21. Copeland, Lewis, *High School Subjects* (Halcyon Press, 1941), p. 114.
22. Copeland, p. 114.
23. Copeland, p. 114.

[24] McDougal, Walter A., *Freedom Just Around the Corner* (Harper Collins, 2004), p. 17.

[25] Jennings, Francis, *The Creation of America* (Cambridge University Press, 2002), p. 11.

[26] Johnson, p. 28.

[27] Johnson, p. 28.

[28] Beard, Charles & Mary Beard, *New Basic History of the United States* (Doubleday & Company, 1960), pp. 29-30.

[29] Taylor, p. 160.

[30] Johnson, p. 33.

[31] Sellers, Charles & Henry May, *A Synopsis of American History* (Rand McNally, 1963), pp. 150-51.

[32] Ver Steeg, Clarence, *The Formative Years* (American Book-Stafford Press, 1964), pp. 92-64.

[33] Taylor, p.186.

[34] Boorstin, Daniel J., *The Americans: the Colonial Experience* (Vantage Books, 1958), p. 19.

[35] Angle, pp. A22-23.

[36] Johnson, p.109.

[37] Sellers & May, p. 39.

[38] Johnson, p.109.

[39] Johnson, pp. 116-117.

[40] *The Invisible Hand: God's Influence in American History, The Rebirth of America* (Arthur S. DeMoss Foundation, 1986), p.45.

[41] Sellers & May, p. 45.

[42] Sellers & May, p. 46.

[43] Angle, p. 83.

[44] Sellers & May, p. 46.

[45] Sellers & May, p. 46.

[46] Sellers & May, p.50.

[47] Gavian & Hamm, p. 107.

[48] Gavian & Hamm, p. 107.

[49] Beard & Beard, p. 109.

[50] Angle, pp. 99-100.

[51] Canfield & Wilder, p. 110.

[52] Miers, Earl Schenck, *History of the United States, Vol. 3* (Golden Press, 1963) p. 213.

[53] Muzzey, p. 95.

[54] Wagenheim, Harold H., Matthew Dolkey & Donald G. Kobler, *This is America* (Holt & Company, 1956), p. 287.

55 Muzzey, p. 95.
56 Muzzey, p. 95.
57 Muzzey, p. 102.
58 Angle, p. 95.
59 Muzzey, p. 105.
60 Wagenheim, Dolkey & Kobler, p. 27.
61 Canfield & Wilder, p. 108.
62 Beard & Beard, p. 113.
63 Muzzey, pp. 115-118.
64 Copeland, p. 121.
65 Miers, Earl S., *History of the United States, Vol. 4* (Golden Press, 1963), pp. 280-84.
66 Carson, pp. 211-12.
67 Canfield & Wilder, pp. 138-40.
68 Hertzberg, Arthur P., *The Jews in America* (Simon & Schuster, 1989), pp. 62-67.
69 Carson, p. 202.
70 Johnson, p. 109.
71 Carson, p. 53.
72 Johnson, p. 194.
73 Carson, p. 428.
74 Levin, Mark, *Men in Black* (Regency Publishing, Inc., 2005), p. 36.
75 Levin, pp. 40-41.
76 Carson, p. 428.
77 O'Neill, J. M., *Religion and Education under the Constitution* (DeCapo Press, 1972), p. 189.
78 Levin, p. 43.
79 Levin, pp. 40-41.
80 Gingrich, Newt, *Winning the Future* (Regency Publishing, 2005), p. 45.
81 Van Dusen, Henry P., God in Education (Charles Schribner & Sons, 1951), pp. 190-91.
82 Uhlmann, Michael M., *The Supreme Court v. the Constitution of the United States of America*, (*Claremont Review of Books, Vol. VI, No. 3*, 2006).
83 Uhlmann.
84 Rawls, Phillip, *Black's Induction into Hall of Fame Draws Criticism* (Associated Press, April 15, 2006).
85 Levin, p. 45.
86 *Rehnquist and Company are Wrong* (*Church and State, Vol. 43, No. 4*, April 1990), p. 24.

[87]   Van Dusen, pp. 189-93.

[88]   Van Dusen, p. 101.

[89]   Whitehead, John W., *The Bible and the Dawn of the American Dream, The Rebirth of America* (Arthur DeMoss Foundation, 1973), pp. 36-37.

[90]   Miller, Dave. *Reason and Revelation, Part I* (June 2006).

[91]   Carson, pp. 23-24.

[92]   Miller.

[93]   Whitehead, p. 70.

[94]   Gross, Martin L., *The End of Sanity* (Avon Books, 1997), pp. 30-34.

[95]   Savage, Michael, *The Enemy Within* (WND Books, 2003), p. vi.

[96]   Codevilla, Angelo M., The Character of Nations (Harper Collins, 1997), pp. 6-17.

[97]   Jacoby, Jeff, *State Religion? What a Pain the ACLU Can Be. (Boston Globe*, May 30, 2006).

[98]   Black, Jim N., *America Adrift* (Coral Ridge Ministries, 2002), pp. 31-32.

[99]   O'Neill, p. xi.

[100]   Levin, p. 52.

[101]   Boston, Rob. *Priority Mail: How President Jefferson's Letter to the Danbury Baptists Changed the Court of Church-State History Church & State, Vol. 55, No. 1* (January 2002), p. 15.

[102]   Wells, H. G., *Mr. Britling Sees It Through* (P. F. Collier & Sons, 1916), p. 503.

[103]   Zangwill, Israel, *The Melting Pot* (1908).

[104]   Gavian & Hamm, p. 86.

[105]   De Tocqueville, Alexis, *Democracy in America, Vol. 11* (Alfred A. Knopf, 1966), p. 23.

[106]   Butts, R. Freeman, *The Public Schools Moral Authority* (*Educational Leadership*, ASCD, December 1977), p. 5.

[107]   *Public Schools are under Assault*, (*Church & State, Vol. 47, No. 6*, June 1994), p. 24.

[108]   Reavis, G. H., *An Educational Platform for the Public Schools*: A Statement of Educational Policy (Prepared with the cooperation of City School Superintendents of Chicago, June 1994), p. 45.

[109]   Martin, Tim, *Michigan Approves Evolution* (Associated Press, October 2006).

[110]   De Tocqueville, p. 335-36.

[111]   Levin, p. 209.

[112]   Levin, p. 202.

[113]   Levin, pp. 195-203.

[114]   *Church and State* (Fox News Documentary, April 2006).

[115]   Falwell, Jerry, *Rebirth of America* (Arthur DeMoss Foundation, 1986), pp. 225-27.

Index

www.ingramcontent.com/pod-product-compliance
Lightning Source LLC
Chambersburg PA
CBHW021240280526
45784CB00005B/2182